Mary Elizabeth Blake, Margaret F Sullivan

Mexico

Picturesque, political, progressive

Mary Elizabeth Blake, Margaret F Sullivan

Mexico

Picturesque, political, progressive

ISBN/EAN: 9783337070397

Printed in Europe, USA, Canada, Australia, Japan

Cover: Foto ©Suzi / pixelio.de

More available books at **www.hansebooks.com**

Picturesque · Political · Progressive

BY

MARY ELIZABETH BLAKE
AUTHOR OF "ON THE WING" "POEMS" ETC.

AND

MARGARET F. SULLIVAN
AUTHOR OF "IRELAND OF TO-DAY"

" Pais querido y hermoso, cuya belleza es conocido solo por sus hijos! Como mereces ser conocido y estimado por todos!" — ANÓNIMO.

BOSTON 1888
LEE AND SHEPARD Publishers
10 MILK STREET NEXT "THE OLD SOUTH MEETING-HOUSE"
NEW YORK CHARLES T. DILLINGHAM
718 AND 720 BROADWAY

THE authors desire to return thanks to the editors of the "Boston Journal," and the "Catholic World" of New York, for their courtesy in allowing the use of articles which had formerly appeared in their columns.

M. E. B.
M. F. S.

COPYRIGHT, 1888, BY LEE AND SHEPARD.

MEXICO: PICTURESQUE, POLITICAL, PROGRESSIVE.

CONTENTS

PART I
PICTURESQUE MEXICO

CHAPTER | PAGE
I — INTO THE SUN LAND 7
II — GLIMPSES OF A NEW WORLD 27
III — THE CITY OF MEXICO 54
IV — THROUGH LANES AND HIGHWAYS 76
V — ON THE SOUTHERN SLOPE 95
VI — SHRINES AND PILGRIMAGES 117
VII — LITERARY MEXICO: A GROUP OF NOVELS . . . 133
VIII — BLOSSOMS OF VERSE 159

PART II
POLITICAL AND PROGRESSIVE MEXICO

IX — FROM CONQUEST TO INDEPENDENCE 173
X — CONSTITUTION AND GOVERNMENT 191
XI — RELIGION AND EDUCATION 199
XII — REVENUE AND ITS APPLICATION 213

PART I

PICTURESQUE MEXICO

BY

MARY E. BLAKE

MEXICO
PICTURESQUE POLITICAL PROGRESSIVE

———•·———

CHAPTER I

INTO THE SUN LAND

In these days, when a passion for travelling has become one of the manias of American civilization, and people seek the excitement of novelty in despite of difficulty and danger, it is not strange to find that fashion so tempers fancy as to set the tides of desire flowing in special directions, while equal or greater attractions are left high and dry outside the current of sentimental regard. Thus it comes to pass, that, where thousands cross the seas to gain a more or less superficial acquaintance with the main points of European scenery, one could reckon within the limits of as many hundreds those who become in any degree familiar with the wonderful beauty which Nature has lavished upon our own land. It is evident that many instincts of love, of remembrance, and of affection naturally go to increase pilgrimages to the shrines of the Old World. But, when every allowance has been made, there still remains an unaccountable lack of curiosity and knowledge concerning that portion of the world which is essentially ours.

This being so, it is small cause for surprise to find near us, united to portions of our southern country by ties of common origin, customs, and language, a land almost unknown, much misunderstood, and wholly misrepresented. A country picturesque beyond description, and beautiful beyond belief; with traditions of the past to interest the antiquarian, and problems of the future to occupy the progressionist; with the fascinations of a strange tongue and a strange people, and with that indefinable charm which those indolent, lotos-eating lands exercise always over the sterner and colder nature of the northman, — Mexico lies among her mountains, almost as far removed from human ken as the Enchanted Beauty before the Prince kissed her sleeping eyes.

Separated from Texas at El Paso only by the

narrow waters of the Rio Grande, one enters Mexico with no more consciousness of change than in passing from one portion of a frontier town to another. Until within a few years the passage was made by means of a primitive rope ferry, with a delicious slowness and uncertainty which were partial preparation for the strangeness beyond. Some taint (or shall we call it tonic?) of Bohemianism there is in most healthy human natures, which creates delight in the unconventional, and makes the pulse throb with excitement at the first escape from routine. At the entrance to a new world, one craves something beyond the practical methods of commonplace, but to-day the triteness of a hackneyed civilization follows one to the very threshold. A jingling little tramway crosses a wooden bridge, and the traveller steps into the streets of El Paso del Norte with the straws and dust of a familiar world still clinging to him. But in a moment it is as if a magician's wand had been raised. He left on the other side of the river the busy, bustling American settlement, thriving but ugly; he enters upon enchantment here. A soft, caressing air woos like mild breath of welcome after the sharpness of a northern February; linnets sing deliciously to the morning; willow withes are turning yellow by the narrow ditches of clear water. Through the brown, dusty plains stretch winding lanes, outlined by high walls of dried mud, behind which shine the rosy glow of peach-blooms, or scarlet-tipped hedges of cactus spikes. Low, flat-roofed, adobe houses fit into the blank wall, relieved occasionally by a heavily barred door, or stand in the midst of bare, dry fields, as cheerless and desolate as they. On each side, shallow streams, brought from the hills or from hidden springs, run in sluiceways which at intervals cross the roadway. Here and there a carpet of delicate green, the drooping grace of a plantation of young cottonwoods, or the checkered squares of a thriving market garden show where the precious water has been freely used; for here, as elsewhere, the most barren tract blossoms at touch of moisture. The field laborers are usually dressed in white cotton, fashioned into short trousers and sleeveless shirts. The women move shyly, covered to the eyes in the long blue scarf, or reboso, which is part of the national costume. Half-naked children, with dark skins and glorious eyes, play about grated door-yards, which open into small patios, or courtyards, beyond, bright sometimes with shrubs and flowers. The men, with wide-rimmed sombrero and gay zarape, lounge or work or walk about with a grave, dark-eyed imperturbability which contrasts strangely with the inquiring vivacity of their class at home. The blank white walls of the old cathedral, with its broken belfry of adobe, rise across the fields; down one narrow lane comes a caravan of enormous covered wagons, each drawn by sixteen mules in bright trappings, and driven by swarth muleteers in costumes that seem borrowed from Carmen. Around another corner dashes a mounted caballero, sitting his small but fiery horse as if the two made but a single creature full of superb motion. The man wears a broad sombrero, brilliant with silver braid; his short, loose velvet jacket is bright with rows of silver buttons, as are also the wide velvet trousers which lose themselves in stirrups of fringed leather. The animal is resplendent in silver-mounted harness, with embroidered saddle heavy with inlaid work; across his neck is thrown a folded blanket of scarlet wool; over his flanks

falls a long fleece of silky black fur. And the
Centaur-like grace of steed and rider flashes
before one's delighted eyes, to disappear as mysteriously again behind the jealous hedges.

Under a mesquite-bush by the wayside one may
see an Indian woman scouring a tall earthen jar,
preparatory to swinging it, fresh filled from the
well, upon her shoulder in the old biblical fashion; under another, a couple of wrinkled crones
are washing clothes in a shallow ditch, and spreading the wet pieces upon the cactus plants to dry.
Now and again a drowsy little tienda shows one
or two unhurried customers at its narrow counter;
or a corner cantine has its inevitable handful of
quiet pulque-drinkers; or a silent brown group,
their glowing eyes alone showing trace of excitement, gathers around a pair of fighting cocks.
The sky above is as blue as Colorado; the air
is pure and sweet, with the softness of a late May
day; and between you and the matter-of-fact,
work-a-day world you left a few hours ago, are
a thousand miles of distance and a lifetime of
difference.

Every step into the new territory to the southward deepens the impression which this first glimpse at people and country makes upon one. The table-lands, separated by long, parallel mountain chains, now approaching and now receding, are full of infinite variety. Aside from the loveliness of the heights themselves, which, rich in mineral dyes and exquisite in outline, make a fresh beauty for eager eyes at each opening of the landscape, a hundred forms of interest and novelty offer a constant series of surprises. It may be a hacienda, — one of those enormous properties covering square miles of country, divided into villages and hamlets, rich in corrals and sheepfolds, watered by streams, luxuriant in gardens and fields of springing wheat. Across the plains, mounted shepherds drive flocks of white silken-fleeced goats and immense droves of cattle; long lines of trees follow the curves of the watercourses; the dome of a church rises amid the foliage; groups of burros and horses follow their Indian keepers through the fields; and the manifold industries belonging to a great and rich estate gather about the central courtyard, with its hollow square surrounded by massive stone buildings. Or it is a break in the hills, through which one looks down into some exquisite valley, deep with purple shadow, faintly luminous with dreamy light, and a glint of water shooting like a silver arrow through the pale green foliage. Or it is a silent city far away on the horizon, its domes and towers tinted in soft shades of pink and blue and warm amber; its tiled roofs flashing; its low gray walls, with masses of drooping trees behind, barely rising from the white level of the plain, like an oasis in the desert. Or it is a forest of cactus stretching for miles in every form of contortion known to this reptile of the vegetable world; or a waste of Yucca palms, each stem tipped by a Hercules club, four feet in height, of waxen lilies; or a plain of unfamiliar flowers, gorgeous but scentless, stretching like a Persian rug to the base of the wonderful heights beyond. Always a sudden change, and each change as splendid as the one before which seemed perfection.

With unceasing difference of detail in color and outline, but the same general peculiarities, these scenes repeat themselves, until the approach to Chihuahua across the wide plain brings us near the first distinctively Mexican city. It lies below the deep purple mountains in the distance; the two tall campanile of the cathedral dominating the landscape, and the low, flat-roofed houses lying upon the terra-cotta surface of the valley with a most Oriental effect. Indeed, every thing about the spot is distinctly Eastern. Across the plain, as one rides from the station to the town, the serapes of the horsemen recall the burnous of the Arab. So does the magnificent horsemanship, as the riders fly over the open country. Inside the city streets, long colonnades of rude Moorish arches outside the houses, offer grateful shelter from the mid-day sun; the outer walls are frescoed in bright blue, yellow, or red; there is a mosque-life effect about the great central domes of the churches. Broad stone seats with high backs, like those in Alma-Tadema's pictures, line the principal streets under soft shadows of fanlike trees; clumps of Mexican aloe and prickly cactus hedge the roadways. There is a barbaric richness of ornamentation about the façade of the principal church, carved in solid stone by, native artists from native designs; but it loses somewhat, upon closer inspection, from its crude conception of art. It is, however, greatly superior to the more tawdry and more insincere decoration of machine-turned woods, to which we are unfortunately too well used in church architecture at home. From the flat roof, a beautiful prospect opens on all sides. A fine row of gray stone arches marks the path of the aqueduct built more than two hundred years ago to convey water from the mountains beyond. A bird's-eye view into the inner portion of the adobe houses near gave an added touch of strange interest to the scenes. A courtyard almost immediately below had a tiled floor, surrounding a garden bright with peach-bloom and century plants. Two shaggy burros and a group of picturesque children played in and out among the heavy stone arches of the open gallery leading to the rooms of the house, which were lightened by vivid frescos of brilliant white and blue. One or two shadowy forms lounged against the pillars of the wall; a woman's voice came singing from the rooms beyond; and a flock of gray doves rose and fell like a soft cloud above the flat roof. Outside, down the long cottonwood-fringed street, three horsemen, one all in white, one draped in deep red, and a third with flying parti-colored sashes, shone like blotches of color against the pale sky.

On the route between Chihuahua and the Plains of Zacatecas, the beautiful mountains continue, now nearing and now departing from the table-like valley between. An entire tract of country at one place is covered thickly with pale purple blossoms exhaling a faint, sweet odor. The great haciendas, lying near the route, have portions of their ranches near the line. It may not be understood, so it is well to explain here, that a hacienda is the large estate of which numerous ranches form part. The owner is supposed to exercise a kindly care over all his assistants and dependants; churches and schools are provided within the limits; in many cases a hospital is conducted for the health and comfort of the laborers, and a somewhat patriarchal system obtains. The peon, or laborer, cannot leave one hacienda for another without the consent of his master, and the pledging of some portion — usually a quarter — of his wages, until his obligation is paid. It is a remnant of an old system of bondage, and will probably give way to progress and time. Some of these haciendas are of immense size; one was pointed out enclosing two hundred and forty square miles.

Across the low, green, rolling foothills the mountains still keep their dusky heights stained with mineral dyes; mines rich in copper, iron, and silver honeycomb the entire country; fine, fertile valleys fill every atom of space that has the blessed luxury of water; and even this is being brought extensively at present, through the medium of artesian wells and springs, from the hills. When one remembers the ditches and flumes extending thirty and forty miles in the California districts, it seems an easy matter to convey it here, from so much nearer sources.

At one or two points, the train stopped to let us load the cars with flowers. A tall cluster of bare rods, each tipped with a vivid scarlet blossom, fine white and purple bells that were found at the root of mesquite bushes, bright little yellow cups like small jasmine buds, and quantities of delicate green soon made our rooms like a travelling greenhouse, and we revelled in bloom and insects until we tired of both. Soon after leaving San Juan de Gaudeloupe, flat, table-topped mountains began to make a change in the landscape. They looked not unlike the old Aztec Teocalli, and might, perhaps, have served the sun worshippers with the idea of their temples. Lofty, terraced sides and level summits extended far enough to allow room for the imposing ceremonial of their worship.

Sometimes for hours, fields green with springing corn, or the soft verdure of young wheat, lined each side of the road; sometimes a herd of sheep gathered about the rare water-courses, or were grouped under great roofs of thatch, held up by forked poles without any side coverings.

Nine miles below the city of Zacatecas, the railroad begins to rise, by a triumph of magnificent engineering, up a grade of one hundred and seventy-five feet to the mile, making on the passage some of the most abrupt curves conceivable. It recalled the old Colorado cañons, only that here we went around the hillside instead of plunging over precipices and bridging gorges with trestles. The powerful engine panted like some hard-pressed animal, and the train of heavy cars dragged wearily up after it. We forgot fatigue, forgot fear, forgot — what is harder to forget than either — supper, and crowded the narrow platforms with an excitement almost painful. At last, with one mighty, final effort, we turned the last sharp mountain spur, and with the Büfa rising high on the left, its enormous crest of rock above like the dorsal fin of some fossil monster, with a glow of red gold over all the western sky, and the evening star shining palely in the east, we rested on the crest of the hill above the dark, little, sleeping town, with only three faint points of light to indicate its location or give any sign of life.

When we passed next morning down the steep slope into the city, a long line of convicts, under direction of an armed guard, were carrying earth upon their backs, in bags, up the side of a long embankment, and into a fortified place above, which was being repaired. Grouped about, and giving the grave attention of idle people to each detail, were a number of Mexican men, women, and children, picturesque in rags and brilliant scarfs. In recognition of a bow in passing, the convicts lifted their hats and showed so many sets of white teeth and gleaming eyes; such a careless, easy-going set of criminals it would be hard to find elsewhere.

The narrow streets were well paved, wonderfully clean, and furnished on one side with raised pavements; open archways looked into little courtyards glowing with sunshine and flowers; cobblers, tinkers, tailors, and jewellers sat at work on raised stone platforms outside their houses; and in the central one of the many market-places, around the great circular stone fountain, a mass of women, girls, and boys dipped the water into great red earthen jars, in little gourd-shaped cups with handles like ladles. Of all the many strange sights so far met, this was by far the strangest. Each one, as her laborious work ended, lifted herself for a moment to straighten the cramped muscles, and then with marvellous ease, for what must have been a real effort of strength, swung the tall jar to its place on the left shoulder, held it in position with the bare right arm, and walked off with as much ease as a ball-room belle in the mazes of a country dance. The clamor, the crowd, the utter absorption of each one in her own work, and the strange impression of life it left upon us, it was impossible to describe. Whether the knot of lounging youths was made up of so many Jacobs waiting for these Rachels at the well, was another question. They showed the true Eastern imperturbability, while the women did the work.

Down a steep side street — every street climbs up or runs down a hill — to the beautiful old church with its monstrous façade of carved freestone and three unique spires, and the covered market with its double rows of open Moorish arches, we passed with new delight at every step. Every thing is glowing with color — the sky deep as Italy, the frescos, the flowers, the fine ash-trees, the brightly dressed people, the broad white stone seats. The inner court of the governor's palace — *patio* is a prettier word, so we will use it hereafter — was finished with dado and frieze of blue and yellow; the slender pillars, rising in a double flight of columns between the arches of the first and second floors, were gay with stencilled wreaths of bright flowers; the broad gray stone steps, curving in wide sweeps to the upper galleries, were dressed with fanciful large pots full of tropical plants. From a corner of one of these shaded upper galleries, a most beautiful picture was made by the three red sandstone towers of the cathedral, — one with the round, flat dome of the mosque, one a slender campanile, and one a solid square, but each a mass of most wonderful stone carving, almost barbaric in splendor, and still kept within the bounds of harmony. Against the glowing depth of sapphire sky, it was superb.

In and out, up and down, there was no end of novelty. One market-place was devoted entirely to the coarse potteries of the place, — jars for water and cooking, table articles and kitchen utensils, all good in shape, with an excellent glaze, and some attempt at decoration. Their fire-proof qualities were tested by hundreds of small fires of mesquite and cedar, which kept them bubbling here and there with boiling soup and vegetables. At the Zacatecano Hotel, for dinner, we had our first experience of real Mexican cookery. A very good onion soup was succeeded in regular courses by steak dressed with mint; a good omelet; rice, prepared with curry, tomatoes and garlic; chicken, in a sort of fricassee; cold tongue, with a dressing of lettuce and eggs; cauliflower; sweet custards; and good but bitter coffee.

We entered this country so incased in barbed points of prejudice that we are, like hedgehogs, bristling all over, and ready to prick against every thing. We have found the people courteous beyond expression. The poorest laborer as gracefully lifts his hat as the high-bred gentleman; and the kindliness of unassuming hospitality opens every house, rich and poor, to the visitor. It is amusing to think what scant politeness a company of strange tourists, curious, eager, and almost impertinent, would receive in Boston and New York. And still, with all our good-breeding, it is so hard to keep New-England noses from curving superciliously at the degraded Mejicano. Are we beyond taking a lesson?

There are a good many that we *might* take, without hurting ourselves. There is the good, honest building, without sham or pretence, which looks as if it were made for eternity. There is the power of restfulness and leisure, which, though unhappily a crying evil here, would be one of the cardinal virtues if we could only ingraft it on our stubborn, rushing, uneasy nervousness. There is their way of holding the dear, dark little babies, with a long fold of the nurse's rebozo, or scarf, wound around the little creature from mouth to hips, supporting the back and neck well, and throwing the child's weight on the bearer's shoulder instead of her arms and hips. And there are the exquisitely clean streets, which would make us blush hot with shame, remembering the filth of Chicago and New York, if our sallow Eastern skins could ever show so beneficent a change of color.

The plan of spending our days visiting or sight-seeing, passing to the next important point in the cool of the evening, and resting luxuriously for the night drawn up on some quiet side-track, works wonderfully well. There is something gorgeous in the idea of a special train, that moves when one pleases and rests when one desires; that goes on like an obedient carriage-horse, stopping here to let you pick flowers, and there for fear of disturbing your after-dinner coffee; that meets you with welcome, homelike face after each new pilgrimage into the strange, unknown country; that offers you plenty of plump pillows and soft cushions to poultice the bruises of fatigue. It is a little nest of such comfort and luxury as these Mexican cities, enchanting as they are as studies and full of brilliant novelty, have not as yet the slightest conception. To come back from a tiresome and exciting ride in quest of pleasure or information; to find your quarters swept and garnished; your neighbors in their customary places; the judge's pretty wards at their knitting or crochet; the blonde-haired Vassar girl sharpening her clever pencil; and Peter, your man-of-all-work, waiting with smiling welcome and a helping hand at the door, — is to know something still of home feeling in the midst of strangeness, and to thank Heaven silently, but emphatically, for the Pullman. Ice-water in the tank, and your slippers on your feet; your books on the table, and a good bright light under which to read them, —these look like trifles to you, O easy-going devourers of the corpulent good things of beloved Boston, but wait till they come to you in Méjico!

CHAPTER II

GLIMPSES OF A NEW WORLD

UNDER a long avenue of superb cottonwoods, the largest we have yet seen in the country, the warm waters which give Aguas Calientes its name flow through a series of really fine baths, well built of a soft red stone, and out again into wide ditches in which the common people wash themselves and their family linen. Irreverent members of the party affected to believe that this order was reversed; but I do not credit it, and so my readers need not. A better class, or a larger number of a better class, than we had found in any town before, made the streets interesting. The moment the people are lifted into the dignity of self-support, that moment they become joyous and hopeful. We saw new birds in the trees of the plaza; a species of large black crow, with a short but pleasant song. The frescos of the houses were more elaborate and brilliant, the fountains better supplied, the squares enclosed in fine stone balustrades, and the stone seats softly tinted. Chance, or perhaps some longing memory of the family doctor at home, led us into a doctor's office here. Imagine a small door set in a large carved gateway leading through a stone archway into a broad, sunny patio. Under an arch at the right, a pair of fine horses champing in their cool stone stalls; under an arch at the left, some pet birds, a couple of tame ducks, a green and gold parrot on the wall, a silver-trimmed saddle with sharp spurs, and a gay riding-blanket hanging beneath it; through an open door, the clean stone kitchen; through another, a stone bedroom with fresh, clean beds; through a third, the office,— stone, too, like the others, — and all opening on the warm, silent courtyard. The room was cool and dusky, tiled, as were the rest; there were bamboo chairs and lounge, a professional-looking desk, a small pharmacy at one end, a table covered with the wonderful feather-work for which the town is noted, in the centre, and a few engravings on the wall. The shuttered and grated window was closed; light and air came through the great inner door, which stood always open.

A feeling of repose and coolness, in delicious contrast to the dusty, glaring, adobe-lined streets outside, stole pleasantly through our travel-worn senses; and one remembered with new pleasure the sentiment of Longfellow in his lines to Mad River, —

> "Do you not know that what is best
> In all this restless world is rest
> From turmoil and from worry?"

Before the Governor's Palace a brace of trumpeters ushered noon in with a blare of silver bugles; in the market-place the fruit-venders were selling baskets of Indian straw with a hundred oranges for seventy-five cents, and tropical fruits of every description from the agricultural districts on the other side of the hills. The air was hot, but pleasant, always delightful in the shade; and between the months of November and April the changes in temperature had been only fifteen to seventeen degrees. If a stirring, competent Northern company should take it into their heads to build a good hotel, and utilize the mineral waters and superb climate, there is no reason why Aguas Calientes should not become one of the great health resorts of the world. It only needs enterprise and steadfastness, — two qualities not uncommon in the East or West of our own country.

Leon, a city of seventy-five thousand or a hundred thousand people, better supplied with water from the numerous wells, and therefore more beautiful with trees and shade, is extremely interesting, as showing the immense stride which steady employment of any form enables the people to make. Almost every house has its hand-loom, worked as in the old scriptural times, — heavy, cumbrous, and slow, but capable of producing wonderfully good results. One part of the city is given to the manufacture of zarapes, the other to that of rebosos. As nine-tenths of the population wear one or the other, the industry is well established. Although one sees telegraph-wires and telephones, sewing-machines and street-cars, even gas and electric lights, the people still cling to the old-fashioned methods of hand-work. How the amount of time and labor represented can be afforded for the small amount asked for the wares, is hard to understand. We found here, also, some good forms of pottery in the market-place. The beautiful Calzado — a triple avenue of magnificent trees, floored with broad red flagstones, and lined with low hedges of orange-trees in fruit and blossom — was a delightful promenade. Figs, pomegranates, and oleanders, of larger size than those even of California, made every inch of ground beautiful, and the warm air was sweet with fragrance.

In the streets here we began to see the mantilla, — the graceful black scarf, either of lace or fine wool, which is pinned over the hair and allowed to fall loosely above the shoulders. The women of all grades have an erect and graceful carriage. The dress for the street among the better classes is almost uniformly black; the Indian women wear any and every thing, but usually an embroidered white chemise and colored cotton skirt, surmounted by the inevitable blue reboso. The large market-place, with its collection of cool arches, and great splashing fountains in the centre, is always an attraction. Green pease, fresh fruits, young beets, small tomatoes, and potatoes the size of marbles, were spread about in what seemed to us interminable confusion, but which no doubt had a method of its own. We could forgive much to a place where we could buy roses in bunches as large as one's head for six-and-a-quarter cents.

The plazas were gorgeous with flowers, and on one side street we found a theatre which read us a moral lesson, — a fine edifice of stone, with a great open vestibule sixty feet square as entrance, filled with flower-beds, a fountain in the centre, and domed with glass, into which opened the wide galleries by four separate flights of broad stone steps. Behind every group of eight seats a latticed door gave egress to the gallery on each of the four stories, so that no possible panic could produce more than a momentary result.

Beyond Leon, the mountains, which for some fifty miles had been receding, begin to advance again abruptly. Beautiful with dusky lights and purple shadows, rising majestically into the pure, deep sky, with fertile plains under high cultivation, and groves of magnificent trees, the country has all the elements of great loveliness in its every-day aspect. Soon the hills fall away again, the perfectly flat fields return, and the track begins to wind about the steeply climbing grade which leads to Silao. The organ cactus, a kind of green New-England fence-paling continued upwards to a height of twenty or thirty feet, becomes more and more common, making almost the only division between the small fields of the natives; another cactus, tree-shaped and brutally ugly, begins to appear in groves, very repulsive, and with leprous-looking bulbs of pale blossoms on the ends of the spiked, fleshy leaves. Along the sides of the narrow-gauge road leading from the main line to Marfil, whence tram-cars lead to Guanajuata, mines begin to dot the mountain-sides, and the quiet hurry of a Mexican business district creeps into the scene. The roads become alive with herds of burros laden with every product of tropic or temperate zone, and shambling solemnly, earnestly, lop-earedly, toward the distant market town.

Quaintest spot and most delightful in the wide world! The little city of Guanajuato — may its name be written in letters of gold! — has succeeded in charming away the small remnant of common-sense which Mexico has left us. Squalor and poverty, open sewers and the highest death-rate on the continent, were powerless to dim its delightsomeness. A walled city among the mountains, a fortified place set upon the side of heights so steep that the houses seem to be fastened to the rock rather than resting on it, and that a misstep on the dizzy uppermost level of the narrow, high-pitched streets would precipitate the unlucky one into the midst of some plaza three or four hundred feet below. A lovely, bewildering spot, full of lanes and archways, and winding, twisted market-places; with a rabble of picturesque people, selling every oddity under the sun, and a screen of matting; with a crossing and interlacing of narrow, paved ways, which give at every ten steps the effect of a kaleidoscope, with a vista of infinite beauty and novelty at each turning. The upper balconies of the many really beautiful houses were gay with bright awnings and marvellous flowers; the old church of the Jesuits was magnificent in fine arches of soft, pink stone, and wonderful carvings fine as strips of lace-work; the overhanging hills toppled against the deep blue sky wherever one turned, and through a hundred different arches, some vision of softly frescoed, slender-pillared inner courts, bright with blossoms and fresh with greenery, flashed out, no matter how swiftly one passed. From the flat roof of the castle or citadel, where long ago the beloved head of the patriot Hidalgo was perched, ghastly and gory, on the scene of his first triumph, a most exquisite view of the city was to be had. The celebrated reduction works of the fifty mines, which have made the place rich as well as beautiful, — great massive, fortress-like structures of gray stone, perched here and there, far up the mountain-sides, with masses of buttresses and arches and loop-holed, stern walls, — filled the background of each picture, look which way one would. Underneath, and around, and above, — for, high as it was, the climbing city climbed higher still, — the fine network of paved streets ran between softly colored masses of buildings, some like pale green malachite, some of delicate pink, some of deep red sandstone, some of creamy white. The amphitheatre of the bull-ring was just beneath us; a large pottery, where immense piles of red glazed ware caught the sun's rays like so many mounds of rubies, was next; the small flower-decked plazas shone like emeralds. It was a collection of precious things.

Down in the busy streets, for it was market-day, a surging crowd of men, women, burros, and mules jostled each other in ceaseless motion.

Such a mixture of commodities running through every class of merchandise, such a strange grouping of effects, such mingling of sharp cries and liquid voices and strange noises, with the chant of the young boys singing in the prison chapel above all, and the deep, wonderful sky looking down to listen! While we were in the plaza, a beautiful flight of birds, a thousand swift-winged atoms, with a dash of warm red on the dark breasts, wheeled and dipped and rose through the clear air with a rhythm of motion that set the scene to music, and so I desire to remember it.

Into this ravishing spot we were whirled without any more warning than the corners of a few sharp mountains spurs could give us, by one of the fiery little mule tram-cars, that tore at a swinging gallop up four miles of steep hillside, around curves as sharp as a thin woman's elbow, with a swarthy conductor blowing his horn like a bronze Triton on the front platform. It was partly its unexpectedness that charmed, and we forgive even the smells of its *carceleria* for the delight it brought us.

Still the East and always the East! The marvellous resemblance between this tropical world and the Orient is a constantly new surprise. The sandalled feet, the white garments, the bright wrappings, the public fountains, the walled streets and roads, the low, flat houses, the stone balconies, the deep sky, the dark, grave, silent people! Yesterday, at the hotel of Zacetano, the landlady under the upper arches of the inner court clapped her hands thrice, and a dark-eyed *muchacho* came noiselessly to her side, received her message, and sped away again through the shadows as silently as if he were a shadow himself. For the outer world and the street, there is the blank wall, the grated window, the bolted door; inside, for the household, the sunny courtyard gay with fountains and flowers, the large open arches throwing grateful shadows over vast, cool rooms, the cordial family life with its treasures hidden from the prying eyes of the multitude. Street-criers calling their wares; fruit-sellers with great trays of luscious unknown sweetness upon their heads; water-carriers with earthen jars slung across the backs of shaggy donkeys; the strange, soft, liquid tones of a foreign language, — is it all near our own land and our own people? Is it not Damascus or Syria, or Constantinople, with the muezzin ready to call to prayer from the gallery of the mosque, and the wandering venders crying through the narrow lanes, "First blush of the hillsides, oh, strawberries!" Out on the *haciendas* the laborers draw water from shallow wells by means of a long pole balanced across two high-forked sticks, and furnished with a bucket at one end. Poured into the narrow furrows which divide all the land into garden-beds, the water flows at will wherever irrigation is required. The farmer ploughs with a primitive implement that is little more than a sharply pointed stick, fastened to the horns of his oxen by an equally primitive arrangement of ropes. The great lumbering wagons, whether made of wood or of closely joined stems of cactus, roll on solid, cumbrous wheels made from a single round of a tree-trunk, and fashioned into shape by hard labor. The bronze-skinned, bare-legged beggar dozing against some crumbling corner of a white adobe wall; the mule-teams with jingling bells, clattering harness, and shouting driver; the horsemen dashing across the glaring plains, swarth and picturesque in their brilliant riding-scarfs, — what is there to remind us of the staid, sober American life, as ugly as it is comfortable?

AN INDUSTRIAL SCHOOL 39

It is all Oriental, even to the barking dogs that howl through the dark streets by night to quicken the footsteps of the wayfarer.

Now and again, amid this bewilderment of romantic effects, some fine example of practical prosperity is found, as in the Industrial School of Guadelupe, a suburb of Zacatecas. This institution was designed for the training of orphan boys, and is supplied with the means necessary for turning out finished workmen in any one of sixteen different trades. The two hundred and seventy pupils are given a good common-school education, together with practical instruction which places the means of livelihood in their hands from the moment of leaving school. Masons, bootmakers, tailors, printers, farmers, carpenters, telegraph operators, were being here prepared for active life, under care of the Government; a primary department, a school for the deaf and dumb, and a general training in music, also entered into the programme of the institution; and the plan as a whole was in such successful and happy operation, as made it the most satisfactory proof of promise for the future we had yet met in Mexico. The children's faces were bright and animated:

employment invariably lifts the people out of the sad and resigned aspect which otherwise seems habitual to them. Indeed, a very short time in the country is sufficient to convince one of the falsity of American views regarding it. We have heard of the people as lazy, which is an absolute mistake. They are often idle from want of occupation; but where idleness may be only a question of circumstances, laziness is an inherent vice. They are not only ready for employment, but anxious to procure it. They work with an earnestness and honesty that shame our slovenly Northern laborers, whose chief anxiety seems to be to accomplish the smallest amount in a given time. Digging in the fields, carrying water, bearing burdens, the Mexicans work without ears, eyes, or concern for aught save the object in hand: they spare themselves no more than if they were burros or horses. We were told that they were dirty, and their towns filthy. We found them dirty, as regards personal cleanliness, in towns like Chihuahua and Zacatecas, where water has to be dipped with a gourd from the basin of a stone fountain, with scores awaiting their turn, or bought from a carrier. But in

Aguas Calientes, where the warm waters which give the place its name run through the ditches, the population was constantly bathing, or washing clothes; and there was no suspicion of uncleanliness. Under the circumstances, a similar leaning toward dirt would be found among our own poor people; while the bath of the rich Mexican is as much a necessity as his morning coffee. The bare, poor houses and narrow cobble-paved streets are always perfectly clean. Every city of any size in the republic is swept each morning with whisk-brooms and dust-pans. Imagine New-York's Broadway or Boston's Washington Street subjected to a like process! But there is unfortunately absolutely no knowledge of sanitary conditions to supplement this fine wholesome sweeping away of abuses. Drainage and health departments are yet in swaddling-clothes. We have been warned about their thieving propensities, and the ingenuity of their devices to obtain unlawful possession of others' goods and chattels. After visiting twenty cities, and wandering at will through strange and crowded quarters; after displaying in market-place and arcade sums of money, which, though small enough in themselves, were relatively large to these primitive people, we have yet to find the first instance of cheating or of theft. Not only this, but some examples of most stubborn and improbable honesty have appeared in our own set of experiences, which in a party of seventy-five must be reasonably large. Is New York or Chicago, where the inhabitants are obliged to chain door-mats to steps, and fasten burglar-alarms to windows, where pickpockets throng the city thoroughfares, and shoplifters prowl about counters under the dazed eyes of detectives, — is New York going to throw the first stone? Or Boston, where sneak-thieves snatch weekly washings from the lines in back yards, and a bundle left for sixty seconds on the seat of a horse-car is gone from sight forever, as completely as the lost Pleiad? Why should we point a blunt moral in Mexico, which could be given a sharper tip in any large city of our own beloved Union?

Every thing unforeseen is possible here. We are walking through the days that follow the Arabian Nights. Each class of the population wears the garb which is the uniform of its occupation. The water-carrier, in armor of leather, bears his heavy jar suspended from a band around the forehead; the ochre-man, stained like a terra-cotta image from head to foot, carries his package of brick-colored clay above his matted, gory locks; the fruit-vender, crying his luscious wares in sudden, shrill monotone, balances his enormous pannier on his head, and steps as airily as if he were beginning a fandango. Under the open arches of the *portales* the crockery merchant sits before his pile of Guadalajara jars and brightly glazed pottery; Indian women carry their double load of baskets and babies with the superb indifference to fatigue which marks their race; dealers in "frozen waters" call their sherbets in prolonged, piercing notes like those of a midsummer locust; sidewalk cooks squat on their haunches beside small fires of mesquite, over which bubble earthen dishes of stewed vegetables, frijoles, or crisp tortillas; and flower-girls surrounded by piles of glowing poppies, pyramids of heliotrope and pansies, baskets of scarlet cactus blossoms, and tangled heaps of superb roses magnificent in color and perfume, fill the atmosphere with brilliant beauty. No wonder the winter world at home looks pale and cold by contrast!

We shall remember Irapuato with love and delight, when the memory of perhaps better places has faded, because there, one hot, dusty midsummer afternoon of March, we bought Indian baskets of woven grass full of luscious strawberries, and reached refreshment and coolness through the base medium of *dos reales*, vulgarly known as a quarter. The state of business enterprise in the country may be gauged from the fact, that while the little town and its surrounding district overflow with this delicious fruit, and are within ten or twelve hours' distance of Mexico, it never has entered any original mind to establish connection between the two points, and bring the country product into the city market. So that while strawberries go begging for customers at Irapuato, customers go begging for strawberries in the capital, and neither finds what it wants.

The guide-books speak of Querétaro as having forty-six churches. If you should chance to be there on Sunday morning, you will think it has at least a hundred and forty-six; that every church has three towers, every tower three bells, and that every bell is cracked. It would be beyond human endurance elsewhere, but the lighter air of this high altitude makes the sound so faint and tinkling that one is more amused than annoyed. Only the clapper is moved in the act of ringing; and one is haunted all through Mexico by a constant vibrant clatter from these petulant tongues, that reminds one of the "damnèd iteration" of the old poet.

Outside the city, in the pleasant sabbath silence, the fine trees of the Alameda tempered the hot air with shadows; and along all the paths, leading as is customary toward the central fountain, hedges of pale pink roses, with the richest perfume we ever found, even in the regal Jacqueminot, lined each side with luxuriant beauty. The courtesy which had made our way easy so far followed us here, and allowed us to revel in great handfuls of these beautiful things, which scarcely showed a gap in their full ranks after the party had satisfied their cravings. We found ourselves, in rambling about, tired enough to rest upon one of the carved stone seats which have been a source of such delight to us in every town and city so far. Soon one of the uniformed police on duty near by approached, saluted, and in voluble, respectful, sweet Spanish, endeavored to make us comprehend that we were in some way transgressing rules. Unable to reach our understanding through the medium of the tongue, he had recourse to pantomime; and it dawned slowly upon our night of ignorance, that the kindly little man desired us to walk about under his guidance to look at the attractions of the spot. He loaded himself with our wraps and impedimenta, lifted his hat again with the bow of a born courtier, and, silent but eloquent, drew our attention to this or that effect, led us here and there through shaded alleys, picked for us now and again an unusually gorgeous rose, and followed with persistent helpfulness to the door of the Pullman. Even the natural conclusion of a "tip" had to be forced upon him instead of being waited for, and we spent a half-hour of deep mental introspection in trying to comprehend how this product of a semi-civilized state should so outrank his prototype at home in every outward sign which goes to mark the gentleman. Imagine the manner in which two plainly dressed, travel-worn, and commonplace foreigners would be hustled out of some prohibited spot in New York or New England, — say, for instance, a seat on the grass in Boston Common, —

and contrast it with the delicacy which made us appear as if we were conferring a favor instead of infringing a law. Truly we have much to learn.

Within the city, the sabbath silence was not so apparent. The native shops, booths, and markets were doing their full business; perhaps a little gayer than usual with branches of flowers and fringes of green palms, but otherwise the same. The crowd on the plazas had a more holiday look; the men's white trousers and shirts fresh and clean, the women's skirts starched and ironed, and all the humble, contented, happy world chewing sticks of fresh sugar-cane, or a tlaco's worth of the small sweet cakes which meet you at every hand's turn through the kingdom. At every door a group of dusky babies, and above it the inevitable mocking-bird in his rustic cage; from the open church porches, the rolling diapason of the organ, and chanting voices of the choir; in the small stone balconies of the windows, crowds of mischievous, chattering, bright-eyed senoritas, gay in the lightest summer dresses, floating ends of ribbon, and softly fluttering fans. The same look of thrift and bright cheerfulness that distinguishes here always town from country life, solely, we are now quite convinced, from its greater opportunities for employment, shows itself clearly. The nature of the people is industrious, but circumstances are against them. We found palms and bananas for the first time growing in the squares, and among the flowers an occasional tree of scarlet hibiscus, like large lilies, absolutely glowing with color. The houses are of more stories and greater architectural pretension on the street side than in any city before; but, while this adds to the appearance of wealth and comfort, it takes away some of the great novelty which has such a fascination to sentimental travellers. The aqueduct, always a beautiful feature in every town, is finer here than usual; the arches, as the level plain dips into the valley, being of remarkable height. The celebrated mills of the Rubio family, which are the only ones of any note in the country, are the boast of the town, and really of great interest from the odd combination of business and beauty, of peaceful employment and martial law, which their walled territory offers. The most notable remembrance they have left with us, however, is that of the young heir of the house, as he came riding across the plain from the town, at sunset, on a beautiful Arabian horse, with saddle and bridle so richly wrought in silver that it scarce belonged to every-day life, and an embarrassment of luxury in the way of trappings that would have weighed upon a less noble-spirited animal. The boy himself, in silver trimmed *sombrero*, yellow buckskin costume with its precious tassels and fringes of shining metal, impassive, handsome face, olive skin, great dark eyes, and small foot high arched as a girl's, looked like some young prince riding through a fairy tale in search of adventure. The dagger-hilt in his silken sash, and the swarthy groom with his belt thrust full of pistols and cartridges riding behind, gave glimpses of some other happenings which, thank Heaven, are rare as fairy tales in our quiet lives, and well nigh as possible. But, if tradition can be believed, they have been only too common here.

But chief of all interests to us in Queretaro was the fact of its having been the scene of one of the saddest pages in Mexican history,— the death of Maximilian. A heavy rain which had fallen the night before made the roads almost impassable with deep, clinging mud on the morning of the day we drove out to the sad little hillside of Las

Campanas. Half way up the stony slope, facing the lovely city which lies on the opposite side of the valley, rich in brilliantly colored domes and towers, with sunny fields and shaded avenues stretching about the course of the small Rio, and the pale, shadowy mountains filling the blue distance, stand the three stone crosses marking the scene of the tragedy whose shadow rests yet on many hearts. On the quiet plain between, in that June dawning, the Mexican army was drawn up to see the last act of the short drama. Even now, twenty years after, one cannot look upon the spot without feeling some faint throb of the intense anguish which must have filled the heart of the chief actor, looking for the last time upon the fair land which had lured him to death. This is neither the time nor the place to enter upon any discussion of the intention or character of Maximilian. He paid for his mistake, if mistake it really were, with his life, as became a man who had the courage of his convictions, and a king who feared dishonor rather than death. But any one who reads the torn leaves of Mexican history from his day to ours; any one who sees the present condition of the timid, patient, long-suffering people; the present status of the revolution-tossed, dispirited country, unconscious of its own resources, ignorant of its own strength, must acknowledge that the problem of right and wrong is more easily stated than answered. The simple earnestness of purpose which he brought to the solution of Mexican politics, his wise foresight, his overwhelming desire for the good of the people and advancement of the country, and above all his love for the work to which he believed himself called by that *vox populi*, which becomes under such circumstances the *vox Dei*, should claim for him lenient judgment and profound pity, even from those at variance with his political creed. With him, beneath the thin veil of imperial power, Mexico would have been likely to feel the protecting warmth of a wise and kind father's love, supplemented by the best counsel which modern science and wisdom can lend to government; as it is, under the title of a republic, she is become the battle-ground for a host of needy partisans, greedy for gain, ambitious for power, and openly parading the worst vices of a military despotism under the stolen name of liberty.

The great advance which has been made during the last few years in the principles and policy of the ruling party, especially since the accession of President Diaz, seems to possess elements of staying power as well as of good judgment; but one cannot help feeling that such an honorable solution of the problem of self-government would have been possible much sooner if the people had known some earlier training in self-respect and the authority of well-meaning rulers.

According to the advice of friends, who warned not wisely but too well, we came into this country armed at all points with munitions of war in the shape of insect-powder, pain-killer, and extract of pennyroyal. We expected every thing, from fleas to scorpions, from mosquitoes to tarantulas; our thoughts by day and our dreams by night were filled with unknown species of Lepidoptera and Coleoptera seeking what they might devour, and usually finding it. But, so far, not a stopple has been touched in any of the bottles provided with such admirable foresight. We have not met more than a fly. We have found absolutely no more vermin than at home, and only a reasonable share of dust; but by way of compensation we have discovered more smells of rare and distinct species than we dreamed this round world could hold. The smells of Mexico are massive and infinitive: they are the only one of her resources which has been worked for all it is worth. According to the principle in natural law, which makes one more readily cognizant of vice than of virtue, we notice the bad odors most now; but by means of that divine system of compensation which makes the memory of evil fade, while that of good lives forever, it is the scent of her rose-gardens, the sweet, evanescent perfumes of her tangled flower-hedges, and thickets of fragrant shrubs, that we will remember during the long Northern days when all this changeful experience shall seem but a midsummer night's dream.

CHAPTER III

THE CITY OF MEXICO

THE country about Queretaro dimples into a nest of sunny valleys, rounded and curved into great beauty, unlike the long plains to which we have grown accustomed; and the fields of wheat have the same delicious Irish green which we saw on entering the country, but which had given way for some time to harsher tints.

At Tula we receive our first introduction to that ancient Mexico which was so strongly impressed upon our minds before being brought face to face with the modern country. To those who have felt the witchery of Prescott's story of its conquest, it is the old world with its shadowy and poetic peoples, its vanished tribes of Toltec and Aztec, its vague, mystical rites, combined of flowers and sacrifice, of tenderness and cruelty, that appeals most strongly to sentiment before entering. But the reality of the present soon asserts its sway; and, except to those most deeply imbued with the passion of the antiquary, it is the new, strange land, and the exquisite novelty of color and interest in which it is set, that command and hold attention afterward. Even here, with the remains of the old gods standing in the sunshine of the small plaza, and the relics of old barbarism in the dust of the Toltec pyramid beyond, one feels more as if he had stumbled upon a new discovery than on the evidence of an old fact. We gathered broken fragments of obsidian razor-blades and flint arrow-heads which had probably known, hundreds of years ago, the baptism of human blood; we saw, in the pavement of the venerable church, stones covered with hieroglyphics belonging to the idolatrous worship of the past. But across the sacrificial hill, flowers were springing, and birds singing in the bright air; on the carved floor before the altar a group of little children offered loving prayer to the Christian's God, and in the evidences of a simpler and purer faith, the gloom of those ancient mysteries was pushed into the background.

It was here on a hill by the railroad that we first saw the process of pulque-making going on in a small plantation of maguey, and tried for the first time the national beverage. If any one has ever tasted or smelled the old-fashioned yeast, which was one of the rising powers of the world before Fleischman's compressed tablets wiped it out, they will have a very good example of this delectable drink. It no doubt has virtues, but they are well hidden; and if, as they claim, one can become intoxicated by prolonged drinking, it is the sourest, thinnest, saddest means of reaching exhilaration that the mind of man ever conceived. Its introduction into any country as a popular stimulant would be better than a Maine liquor-law. It is one of the articles for which that ugly English word "nasty" was intended.

And here, too, for the second time, we were introduced to the well-bred society of convicts. They were sweeping the streets with the inevitable small hand-broom, and returned our salute with the same smiling grace as their brothers at Zacatecas. I am not sure but that the Mexicans have come nearer than we to a solution of one problem, if they can punish a man satisfactorily for a breach of law or gospel, and at the same time allow him to retain his self-respect.

For, after all, what should be the test of the amount of coercion or control which law has a right to exert over individual liberty? Does it desire the moral death of the sinner, or that he be converted and live? Should the main purpose of punishment be retaliation against a criminal, or reformation?

Drawing near any one of the great American cities, the traveller meets little to impress him with his approach to a centre of wealth and power until he reaches the immediate suburbs; or, if the entrance be lengthened, it is more like that of a back way than a front portal. It is the tattered fringe of the imperial mantle, the spots of blemish and dirt which gather in the wear and tear of mighty interests, that first meet the eye, strained to catch a glimpse of the beauty beyond. A utilitarian age and a business people have neither time nor money to waste on fine settings for the jewelled centres of their wealth and power. Prosperity is the touchstone of beauty; having that, they care for no other. The Midas touch which transmutes every thing it reaches into gold cannot spare such simple things as hedgerows and lanes, which add only treasures to the soul, and none to the pocket.

Fortunately for the sentimental traveller, — as he who looks through the world for pleasure instead of profit may well be called, — this fair southern country has not yet been aroused to such sense of its importance as to require the sacrifice of its luxurious, unconscious loveliness upon the altar of interest. Twenty years hence, no doubt, there will be smoky piles of manufactories and workshops, teeming hives of tenement-houses, noise and confusion of traffic and travail, outside the City of Mexico; and it will be a goodly sight to see, since all these are but outward signs of inward thrift. But the glory of Ichabod will have departed. Now the approach to the capital begins thirty miles away. Beautiful and changeful still, in valley and plain and climbing mountain-tops, the consciousness of a new influence begins to force itself upon the senses. The country roads become broad avenues, winding between rows of massive cottonwoods through flourishing fields. The boundless tract of level land begins to show signs of more careful cultivation; water flashes everywhere in the sunlight; velvety green meadows take the place of parched and dust-covered plains. Hedges of century plants and numberless green shrubs divide the different crops in the long panorama of vale and hillside; great plantations of maguey extend into the far distance and even up to the undulations of the foothills, and everywhere fertility spreads the promise of abundance. Bridges and aqueducts, rivulets and ditches, open flume and covered sluiceway, distribute the bounteous, life-giving power all over the land, which teems with rich harvests in return. Soon across the clear air, beside a mass of soft white cloud, — themselves two snowy clouds lifted into the blue of heaven, — the summits of Popocatapetl and Ixtaccihuatl rise in their sublime beauty. Unlike the great peaks of Colorado and New Mexico, which spring almost invariably from a barren and forbidding country, torn and devastated by the same force which caused the primal upheaving, and bearing still its sombre impress, these beautiful forms, wonderful in color and majesty, tower above a world as beautiful as themselves. The exquisite valley takes now a thousand shapes of loveliness. Tropical vegetation shows itself sufficiently to make the landscape rich and bounteous; the quaint, unusual architecture of town and village rising in the midst of strange woods; the softly tinted outlines of mosque and tower; the dark-skinned, white-robed people thronging the roads, — all go to enhance a scene which even without those wondrous heights would be one of fascination, but which with them surpasses the power of words. When at length the stately spires and domes of the great city, glowing with varied color, and its rich Oriental mingling of white walls and arches, are set in the foreground, surrounded by trees and gardens and fountains, the picture can be compared to nothing else. The world holds few scenes to equal it, and none to surpass.

The streets of Mexico are, in a measure, unlike those of any other city we have so far visited. Straight, wide, and lined with handsome houses two or three stories high, almost invariably built of stone, and lighted by large windows opening upon small stone balconies, it loses something of the Eastern character which their narrow lanes of blank adobe walls give to the lesser towns; but it gains a corresponding richness. These little balconies, ornamented often by carvings and always by balustrades of wrought iron, brightened by gilding and color, and shaded by linen awnings, make a feature in themselves. Here on Sunday and *fête* day, as well as toward evening, the youth of the city gathers, in the full dress of private life; and the stolen glances, which form the only intercourse allowed between the sexes, flash back and forward between youth and maiden. Even deprived of the opportunity for interchange of vows, for hand-clasping, and tender greeting, it is self-evident that a young Mejicana, true to the traditions of her Castilian forebears, can make as much havoc with her languishing dark eyes, and the softly fluttering fan which supplements them, as any other girl arrayed in the full rational outfit of courtship. This is true, of course, only when she, as she always should be, but less frequently is, happens to be beautiful. The pretty girls are exquisite: the slender oval of the face, the rich olive of the cheek, the long, sweeping dark lashes over superb eyes glowing at once with passion and tenderness, the low forehead with its rippling mass of dusky hair, the slender neck, the lithe form, the springing step, and the dainty foot, make them like a poet's dream of darkly brilliant loveliness, not to be measured by any type with which we have been heretofore familiar. But Nature is never over-lavish, and the number of these splendid creatures is as few as their perfections are many. Remembering the streets at home after the Friday-afternoon rehearsal, filled with the fragile, flowerlike bloom of winsome but delicate girlhood, its brave eyes looking the world full in the face with that mixture of innocence and boldness which is the hybrid blossom of modern civilization, these shy but rich specimens, as rare as they are wonderful, look few indeed. Their perfection is offset by an equally pronounced ugliness on the part of the many; and young womanhood changes into faded middle age even sooner than with us, — which is saying a great deal. Nevertheless, the graceful lace mantilla, which is yet almost universally worn in the street, but which unfortunately is beginning to give way among the better classes to the ugly stiffness of the French hat and bonnet, gives to many a plain face such a soft and effective background that one brings back from a walk only a piquant and pleasing impression. If the Mexican women knew what they were about, they would cling to this becoming head-dress as they do to their faith; the sex has no right to set aside such a charming accessory.

The large and well-paved avenues cross the city at right angles, overflowing with shops of every description, well stocked, and for the most part conducted by French and Germans. Native traders offer their wares under the *portales* and in the open market-places, which are to be found in every quarter. Nothing in the city is of greater interest to the stranger than these crowded and seemingly disordered piles of merchandise, attended by groups of swarthy merchants, men and women, who regard with the indifference of entire disinterestedness your attempts at barter, and show their contempt for ordinary business principles by charging a tlaco or two more at wholesale than at retail. You may take up every article in their stock, and pass the treasures about from hand to hand, without the least sign of apprehension or importunity on their part. The bright foreign air gives to even the smallest lane an interest and novelty. Every occupation has its distinctive mark in dress, which is like a class badge; and this, with the varying costumes of Indian, Spaniard, Mexican, Frenchman, and

American filling the narrow pavements, gives constant variety to the swaying crowd. Anywhere along the curbstone, native men or women sit down to rest with basket or bundle; and some of the groups thus made are exceedingly picturesque. Each long vista, gay with color and life, is closed at last by some towering mountain height, which frowns or smiles as sun or shadow rests upon it. There are fewer burros, those pariahs among civilized beasts of burden, but more horses and elaborately equipped private carriages. A host of hacks, marked by small red, green, or white flags for convenience in hiring, are in the plazas and at street-corners; and a much larger proportion of people use them than in American cities. Small wonder, when a carriage for four people need cost but fifty cents an hour.

The Iturbide is a good specimen of the best Mexican hotels, — larger and finer than most, on account of its original use as the palace of the old emperor, but following the same general plan. Entered from the street by a large archway, the house rises around a fine courtyard, upon which each of the four stories opens in a succession of galleries, supported by arches and pillars of stone.

Every room has a great hinged window opening to the floor, and entering directly on these airy, shaded balconies. Over the casements and corridors leading to the state apartments, elaborate carvings ornament the heavy stone trimmings; and projecting from the flat roof, with long gutter pipes of metal protruding from their grinning mouths, a row of grotesque gargoyles, of great size and striking artistic effect, surround the four sides. Other arches open in three directions on other courts, and broad stone stairways lead to the upper stories. The rooms, opening usually by one great balconied window on the street, as well as on the inner courts, were large, charmingly cool, well furnished, and scrupulously clean; the beds, which frightened us at first, being laid Mexican fashion on two-inch planks for springs, vindicated themselves by giving nights of restful sleep; and the chambermaids, who were all chamber men, were the most helpful, kindly, attentive, delightful set, without any exception, it was ever our happy lot to know. We had grown used to the usual American article, who answers the bell with the look of a martyr, and does your bidding with the air of a churl; who sourly fills the letter of his contract, and patronizingly accepts the timid *douceur* you offer as a sop to Cerberus. We were amazed by meeting a race of beings who anticipated needs, and suggested luxuries; who were interested in your night's sleep and your morning aspect; who were grieved over your ailments, and sympathized with your loneliness; who were always within call, and whose bright, dark eyes showed that they had a joy in the service they rendered. Open doors, and the careless disorder of forgetful travellers in leaving money and valuables about, offered no temptations to an integrity as incorruptible as their other virtues. Over and over again we were met by such evidence of this as would call for special mention in other places, but which here was an every-day occurrence. The lost art of honesty seems to have been found again in Mexico. And this was among the people against whom we had been warned as a race of born thieves, and specialists in the profession of robbery and trickery. We were a party of seventy-four; we had come, as most people do, with preconceived notions gathered from men and books; so that I am the more happy in being able to record this total difference between our experiences and expectations. It is a simple act of justice that it should be placed at least side by side with opposing statements. And the *cameristes* of the Iturbide — be their memory blessed — were the last straws that broke down our camel's hump of prejudice. In my special case, even the shock of finding my maid a man, and the man's name Jesus, could not shake my comfort and delight in him.

So far, in this country, society seems to have builded with the ruins of its old institutions: the stones of broken monarchies have been used to raise the edifice of the new republic, which has, as yet, added little fresh material of its own. It is still, as its enemies sneeringly call it, the land of to-morrow; the attempt at progress is constantly nullified by the habit of procrastination; and the best-laid plans for improvement in business are frustrated through ignorance of the value of present action. Unhappily, those in authority lend themselves to this weakness, instead of combating it by precept and example. The methods of government are as uncertain as those of trade: it is no more likely that a law which has been placed on record will be enforced, than that your merchant will fill his contract within a specified time, — which, indeed, is a small accident, that happens occasionally in better regulated communities. But here uncertainty seems to be the one fixed principle: it is only the unforeseen that ever happens.

During one of the early days of our stay we drove out to an old Carmelite convent, deserted since the action of the Government, twenty or twenty-five years ago, which confiscated all church property to the State. It was the Feast of St. Joseph; and wayside shrines were bright with flowers, laid before the beloved feet of the Virgin by reverent hands. These little nooks, which bring a thought of heaven and heaven's rest into the midst of the busy streets and the hurry of every-day life, seem to me a gracious and beautiful thought. Why would not an occasional one be a good exchange for Coggswell fountains and similar ornaments in the world at home? The celebrated tree of the Noche Triste, under which Cortez passed that "Sad Night" so memorable in the History of the Conquest, was one of the landmarks, with the small church close by, which was among the earliest buildings erected by the Spaniards. Across the lovely, dusty country, the faint line of blue mountains rose through the unusual mist of a foggy day, with Popocatapetl like a restful shadow beyond. Farther yet, the white lady Ixtaccihuatl lay sleeping in her dreamland of clouds. Up and down the long, shaded alleys inside the convent walls, with water running through stone aqueducts, and springing through small fountains at the side; with roses, tangled and fragrant, making hedges under the trees, and a pair of tame goats gambolling through them, — we walked for hours through the ruins of a once splendid property. The fine old building, with its long corridors and frescoed walls, had been turned into a carelessly kept barn and granary; a couple of horses had their stalls under the painted ceiling of the refectory, and in the cloisters still remained the presses and vats used for making oil and wine. Outside, an Italian terraced walk of faint pink stone surrounded a small artificial lake, reflecting a long colonnade of light columns supporting an elevated promenade above. Great clustering bushes of pink roses bent above the water at each few feet; apples, peaches, quinces, and pears grew side by side with oranges, lemons, figs, and olives; and we wandered about for hours, filling ourselves with fancies faint and sweet as the perfume of faded flowers, and gathered armsful of bloom, until we looked like visitors at a country fair. And we could not help speculating upon the common-sense of a nation, which, having taken the very positive step of expelling religious communities in order to increase the revenues of the State by utilizing their properties, should leave these same properties go to ruin for twenty years, without any further effort to make them available. It is another one of the hieroglyphics of this untranslatable country.

There is no end to pleasant surprises. We wandered into a pleasant corner one day. It was a long, narrow garden, with oleander-bordered paths, and a row of rustic pavilions on one side, holding baths of clear water upon floors of shining marble, into which one descended by a couple of broad steps like those in a Pompeiian picture. The walls were covered with a network of fragrant growing plants; and outside, in the trellised arbors, birds were singing, as if harmony and beauty were the only laws of life. On the other side, an archway led to baths for horses, which were novel and pretty enough. Think of equine aristocrats, who have first a courtyard full of clean dust to roll in; a preliminary swimming-tank to flounder about in; careful attendants, with soap and brushes, to shampoo mane and tail, and to wash teeth and ears as if they were caring for babies; and a regal pond of clean water to finish their ablutions, from which they emerge shining, sleek, and beautiful as the winged steeds of Parnassus. Good horses, when they die, must go to Mexico.

If the journey through the country, with its immense preponderance of poor dwellings and adobe huts, should have tended to make you believe that this is the native land of poverty, take a drive any evening, from five to seven, along the Paseo which Maximilian planned from the walls of the city to the Castle of Chapultepec. A boulevard three miles in length, and two hundred feet in width; with double avenues of fine trees shading wide stone sidewalks; with seven great circles, each three hundred feet in diameter, breaking its long, level straightness, — it makes a fit setting for the brilliant display it holds. The centre of each circle is to be filled with a monument or statue, surrounded by a garden with fountains and flowers, around which on each side the avenue sweeps superbly. But a land cannot have too many pastimes; and the favorite one here, of revolution, checks such minor matters as internal improvement and decoration, so that only three of these pretty pleasure-grounds have been finished in twenty years: the other four are as yet in outline. Through this magnificent driveway hundreds and hundreds of brilliant equipages pass and repass in the late afternoon, — the carriages full of brightly dressed ladies, the servants in splendid but showy livery, and the *jeunesse dorée*, more gilded than ever under this Oriental sun, dashing on their small, fiery steeds through the central space. The young girls wear flowers in their dark hair; the elders drape head and shoulders in the soft black lace of the mantilla, which adds a new grace to even a homely woman; the cavaliers are valiant in all the picturesque bravery that youth can dare or money purchase; and a gay whirlwind of nods and smiles, and that fascinating little Mexican greeting which is spoken with the fingers, blows away forever your idea of undiluted misery. For two hours, at least, each day, the world of fashion, of folly, and perhaps of pleasure, has its own way; and it is as giddy a way as wealth can make it. On Sundays and *fête* days a band adds very good music to the other attractions of the place, the reckless riders dash between the lines of carriages more madly than ever, the air is heavy with the perfume of flowers carried in every hand, and nothing more brilliant can be well imagined.

At the farther end of the Paseo, on the road to Tacubuya, rise the hill and palace of Chapultepec. The favorite pleasure-garden of Montezuma, this lovely spot owes its mixture of wildness and beauty as much to art as to nature. Rising abruptly on the side toward the city from the perfect level of the plain, it is surrounded by a forest of cypress, which is not surpassed for magnificence on this continent. The grand old trees, most of which must date back over twenty centuries, rise in sombre majesty above those of ordinary growth, interspersed among them, like a race of giants towering amid pygmies; and the dim aisles beneath their lower branches are made still more beautiful by the almost intangible softness of draperies of gray moss, festooned and swaying from limb to limb. Through this wood, shadowy as twilight even at midday, the carriage-road winds and mounts to the summit, whereon the castle and military academy are built. And standing on the terrace from which these arise, one looks for the first time across the Valley of Mexico.

In the natural order, there is nothing more wonderful than this scene for loveliness in the wide world, — nothing more calculated to intoxicate the soul with the simple glory of living, since earth still holds such beauty for eyes of man. How can one ever hope to bring before the sense that has not known it that fair green plain stretching from the marble terraces of Chapultepec forty miles away to the dim horizon? How paint that foreground of majestic cypress-trees, draped in shadowy moss, which adds an intangible softness to the dim forest aisles beneath; the long, bright fields of a valley fair as a dream of paradise, divided by hedges of shrubbery or walls of cactus, until the surface resembles an inwrought tapestry of emerald interwoven in myriad gradations of tint; the waving hedges, outlining country roads that fade in the azure distance; the magnificent avenues of stately trees, converging from every point toward the walls of the great city? The city itself, a mass of towers and spires and glowing, richly tinted domes; the scores of villages embowered in leafage, and nestling within shadow of the foothills; the sparkle of water on the distant lake; the grand stone arches of gray aqueducts crossing the country from the heights beyond; the wonderful encircling line of mountains, deep with amethystine shadow, that stand like guardians of the happy valley's peace; and farthest away, but most omnipresent of all, the eternal majesty of Popocatapetl and Iztaccihuatl, cleaving the blue and silent air, lifting their radiant white summits like luminous clouds up to the very gates of heaven, awful in sublimity, as if belonging to the supernatural world, yet tempered with the tenderness of earthly beauty, — who can paint the surpassing glory of this entrancing scene for eyes which have not been touched by itself with the anointing chrism of vision? If no more of beauty than this one view can give were added to one's inner consciousness, the journey to Mexico would be fully requited.

CHAPTER IV

THROUGH LANES AND HIGHWAYS

THE hill of Chapultepec, abrupt enough to assure one of its partly artificial origin, rises some two hundred feet from the valley, crowned by a marble castle, first built under the direction of Maximilian, and now restored for the occupancy of the presidents. Rather tawdry in aspect as one looks up from below, it develops into great beauty on nearer approach. A double row of light and elegant arches in white and pale-tinted marbles supports broad colonnades, from which the main body of the palace springs into the air with an effect of great delicacy and beauty. All the rooms open on these marble balconies; and on the very upper flight, reached by an exquisite stairway with gilded balustrades, have been built fountains and terraced gardens, enchanting as the hanging gardens of Babylon. Around under the arches, the walls have been painted in fine copies of Pompeiian frescos and Greek designs, executed with great purity, both of color and form. This flowery arbor, perfumed and beautiful, thrust up, as it were, into the air, forms the centre around which the rooms of the palace cluster. These are airy, harmonious, fitting for the purpose of summer residence, and contain some marvellous ceilings, wherein Cupids play among tangled flower-wreaths, or blow on conch-shells to waken sleeping Love. The lower story is hardly as fine as the upper, but the wonderful outlook makes it all royal.

Adjoining the palace, the military academy, a sort of Mexican West Point, gave us a passing opportunity to note the system of instruction provided by Government to prepare its future soldiers and scientists. The course reaches over eight years, and qualifies its graduates, either as officers or engineers. The school seems well conducted, with extreme cleanliness and care; the gymnasium fairly large and well attended, the chemical department supplied with a small but choice apparatus, the drawing-school remarkably good, and the sanitary details in dormitories and dining-halls well carried out. The boys, who enter at fourteen or sixteen, were bright, active fellows, proud of the school, self-respecting without being conceited, and as well bred as young gentlemen anywhere could be. Nearly all spoke more or less English; but, as the last four years' courses are conducted entirely in French, they use that language with an ease and perfection of accent that leaves one in doubt as to their nationality. Perhaps some tacit jealousy prevents their honoring the speech of their next neighbor and whilom conqueror with a place in the curriculum; but it will be strange if this little pique long outlasts the advent of the railroad. The pleasure of the young men in showing their school was only equalled by their enjoyment of our appreciation, and both made a happy mixture of genuine enthusiasm. A fencing-bout given for our entertainment showed extraordinary skill, and I couldn't help wishing the dear sophomore at home might see what Southern vivacity could ingraft on Northern science. It is hard to confess, but — Harvard would be obliged to go to the wall.

The world here, the novel, picturesque world, which seems to belong to some other solar system than ours, leaves such an impression of absolute difference on the mind that even familiar objects put on an unusual expression. You see French bonnets and dresses as unmistakably Parisian as if Felix's monogram were embroidered on the side panel; but the olive cheeks, flashing eyes, and slender figures they adorn change the well-known costumes as if they were disguises at a masquerade. You see gentlemen in the ugly attire which fickle fashion has made the exponent of modern civilization; but they look as unlike matter-of-fact English or business-built Americans as the water-carrier in his leather harness, or the mozo in zarape and sandals. Is that a commonplace horse-car dashing around the sharp corner yonder, with two mules on a jingling gallop, swarthy Indian women smoking at the windows, and a conductor blowing his tin fish-horn like a madman? What is the time-annihilating telephone doing in the corner of this drowsy courtyard under the gray quiet of arches that shadow the unbroken rest of centuries, in this land of procrastination and delay? And of all conceivable anachronisms, what brings a nineteenth-century steam-roller into these fifteenth-century streets, where the paving-stones are still brought in from the quarries on men's backs, and the gravel carried from the pits in sacks on men's shoulders? Even the electric lights at night have an eerie look. They were always unnatural, with their cold white glare and frozen sparkle; but they are a thousand times more unnatural here, glittering above a people and a country as primitive as if the world were a thousand years younger. Those pale candles, like farthing rushlights, that disturb the dark no more than so many glow-worms — they are the Lights o' Mexico for the present.

It is the common people who are the principal interest to the traveller. Clinging yet with Indian pertinacity to ancient customs, following, even in dress, traditions two or three hundred years old, they seem as removed from the pressure of changeful events as the fossil remains of another age brought into the light of day. They work with what might be called passion, so intense is their application to any assigned task. But that over, the relapse into stolid indifference is as complete as before. Good or bad, the gentle, trusting, superstitious, timid, easily yielding nature of the ancestors is continued in the descendants. They could be led to noble ends : they have been driven to base uses. Ages of misrule and oppression have not broken their sweet kindliness of soul, or dulled the instinctive courtesy of loyal devotion to a superior. There is every thing to hope for when this people can be roused to a proper understanding of its own importance, and of the threads of advancement lying useless now in their idle hands, but ready to be woven into strong warp and woof of progress.

The seeming unconcern which makes life, both in and out of doors, as open to observation as the air or the sunshine makes them a constant study. One may contemplate manners and habits as if there were no human interests beneath. But, in spite of this outward indifference, a very strong vein of national spirit runs through the people. Hidalgo, Morellos, Guerrero, Juarez, only names to us, are to them living embodiments of vital truths never to be forgotten, brave lights of patriotism and principle that no rain of blood or terror can quench. It is a pity of pities that seventy years of struggle have brought them no nearer freedom of thought and action than they are to-day; still, to have kept alive the impulse of liberty is an immortality for the brave men who died at its altar. In the plazas of many towns rise the monuments to their memory, and the cause they championed: "Tacubuya a sus Martiros," "Chihuahua a Hidalgo;" and the eagerness with which these are pointed out to-day makes the moral plainer.

The city overflows with public buildings of rare interest, both intrinsically and for association's sake. The National Palace contains among its treasures the portraits of the earlier patriots, and the State apartments of Maximilian and Carlotta. Republican and Imperialist alike fell before the fortunes of war, and it is fitting that their relics should be preserved together. An attempt at a practical illustration of liberty is made by allowing every one to enter certain rooms freely. We saw two old women utilizing the principle by smoking very bad cigarettes in the outer reception parlor. In the pretty patio of the museum, the Aztec stone of sacrifice, and some fairly preserved specimens of the ancient gods, move you to a faint understanding of what the far-away, shadowy age meant. The art-gallery held a few really great pictures, among many of less repute. Among the native artists, imagination as yet seems to have taken hold of nothing characteristic of the time or country. This is the more to be regretted, since the land overflows with lavish beauty, and offers wonderful opportunities. So far, the genius of the place has made no particular impression; and the treasures of nature have been passed by for conventional representations of Scriptural subjects of no value. When will a Fortuny or a Gérome arise for Mexico?

Puebla and Mexico, the two principal centres of the country, share more than other places the cosmopolitan character of European cities, as well as the extremes of riches and poverty. While nothing is more superb than their palaces, few things are more squalid than the huts of the poor. The homes of the rich are on a magnificent scale of luxury. An arched driveway leads from the street to the central courtyard tiled with marbles, bright with flowers, statues, and splashing fountains, surrounded by all the appliances which wealth can suggest to indolence. Around this inner pleasaunce the house rises in a series of light-arched galleries resting on carved pillars, communicating by broad outer stairways of stone, and opening into every room by windows and doors of plain or stained glass. Vines and hanging-plants cover the low stone balustrades; gilded cages of mocking-birds and parrots snare the sunshine under the cool arches; and inside the broad, dimly lighted salons and chambers, whatever luxurious taste can bring to aid comfort is lavishly supplied. A host of servants divide among them those more personal services which our rigid aristocrats prefer to render themselves, and a clap of the hands brings instantly a swift and silent attendant. Below, under the arches, on the ground floor, horses stand in their open stalls; there are carriage-rooms, storehouses, and servants' quarters: so that, when the great gates leading to the street are closed, all the elements of luxurious living are complete within. And yet not all the elements: these lavish establishments lack many things which we have been taught to consider necessary for even moderate comfort. Neither grates for fire in the tingling mornings and nights, nor hot-water pipes, nor set-bowls, nor spring-beds, nor kitchen-ranges, nor scores of other common helps, belong to the magnificent *ménage* of a Mexican nabob. As a partial recompense, their women do not break down before thirty-five with nervous prostration. There is no cloud without its silver lining.

The very poor live within four walls of dried mud, on a floor of the same material. Anywhere upon this a fire of mesquite fagots may be kindled, to cook the universal tortilla, which forms almost the sole food of a large class. A few crockery utensils for cooking and eating, a handbrush for sweeping, some water-jars and baskets, perhaps a bundle of maguey fibres for a bed, and the furniture is complete. The zarape is cloak by day, and covering by night; the smoke flies out of open door or four-paned window, as it listeth; the floor is at once chair and table; and that is all, — or rather, it is not all; for with it stay patience, kindliness, and content, three graces hard to account for with such meagre plenishing.

The churches of the country are always a delight in their outer elevations. A strange mixture of the Italian, Moorish, and Gothic, they still preserve a quaint harmony of design, which greatly assists in accenting the picturesque beauty of the country. The loving labor which makes the façades almost invariably exquisite with fine carving, the delicate hues of the softly tinted stone, the domes covered with burnished tiles of pale or brilliant color, the fretted and soaring shafts of belfry and tower, set like mosaics against the sapphire sky, are revelations to the artistic sense. The interiors rarely carry out the promise of the exteriors. A crudity of color in the glaring decorations makes itself felt within, which is dissipated by the largeness and glow of the outside atmosphere. In many cases some false canon of art has caused the original stone carving of the walls to be covered by wretched prettinesses of stucco; but the revival of better taste is beginning to demand a return to the earlier purity of design. Silver railings and candelabra about the sanctuaries, rare tapestries, and paintings by the old Spanish masters, enrich many; but their effect is often spoiled by the immediate neighborhood of poor and tawdry ornamentation. Still, with all its incongruities, the *ensemble* is forcible and picturesque. The high altar rises always under the great central dome. Connected with it by a wide central aisle is the choir-room, placed in the nave between two great organs, rich in carven woods, and screens of wrought metal. A dim light filters down from small windows, set high in the lofty walls. From dawn to dark the slow monotone of the Gregorian chant floats in alternate antiphon and response between the robed priests within the sanctuary, and scarlet-gowned, shrill-voiced choristers, half hidden behind tall music-stands. The people, reverent and silent, glide in for a moment's prayer in the pauses of the day's duties; and a certain mystical atmosphere of religious solemnity, which seems to belong by right to the place, forces itself upon the most material nature. The great cathedrals of Puebla and Mexico reach naturally the highest expression of artistic merit, being magnificent in proportion, and richer even than usual in carving and bas-reliefs.

It is Sunday morning in the City of Mexico. The air is filled with the thin tinkling of innumerable bells; and, guided by their stridulous call, the streets swarm in every direction with a church-going multitude. The strange, overpowering smells of the sewerless city are masked for the time by the fragrance of flowers in the hands of every passing woman and child, — flowers massed in the arms of street-sellers, flowers stacked on the corners and gateways of courts waiting for customers; such roses as never were known outside the Persian Gulistan in long-stemmed dewy bunches; such pyramids of pansies and heliotrope; such tropical gorgeousness of glowing hibiscus and scarlet poppy thrown away for a song or a miserly *real*, which is cheaper than a song itself. Where do you find the bird voice now that will warble for twelve and a half cents? Out of the great doors of the cathedral, and out of the gateways of the other hundreds of churches, the crowd whirls in a maëlstrom of entering and departing waves, as some one of the different services going on within commences or closes. In the bright, warm air, the sunny plaza is radiant with overflowing life; the shrill cries of the merchants make tumult in your unaccustomed ears; every branch of business seems to have received new impulse from eager groups of buyers, in the clean white shirts and stiff skirts that mark holiday raiment. Across through the trees the white tents of "Aguas Nevades" venders advertise the coolness of their frozen waters; the Indian basket-women are dozing in the midst of their mountainous piles of willow ware; the melon and fruit sellers come and go through shaded paths, with trays of luscious sweetness and color balanced upon their erect heads; and even the dark, solemn-faced children dimple into subdued laughter as they munch the *dulces* which no one is too poor to buy. Here and there a *mozo* and his sweetheart walk contentedly hand in hand through the broiling sun, or nestle closely together in the corner of one of the great high-backed stone seats, always either eating or smoking. From the stand in the centre, the band plays its gayest strains; for music here seems to be one of the component elements of happiness. The giddy, dashing small mule-cars, which make up in speed the slow gravity of the rest of the world, spin around one corner to Tacubaya, and another to San Cosmo, and a third to Los Angels: the first class filled with respectable commonplace; the second with a picturesque medley of gleaming teeth and eyes, of bright zarapes and blue rebosos, of positive dirt and superlative happiness. Both classes smoke; all classes smoke; high and low, old and young, clean and filthy, in door and out, every one, everywhere, and always. Perhaps it is because they are carried away by the ruling passion for smoke, that they persist in making their little fires of mesquite on the floors of their huts, and ignore chimneys. The city seems alive with humanity. In open window and balcony, in door and arch way, in plaza and lane and courtyard, the every-day numbers are increased threefold, and the houses have emptied themselves into the streets. The larger shops, being principally conducted by French or Germans, are closed; but the native *tiendas*, the markets, the *cantines* and *pulquerias*, and the omnipresent *candaleria* are widely open. After mass in the morning is the approved time for shopping among the Indians. The man buys his new sandals, and the woman her new veil; and around each purchaser gather the sisters, the brothers, the uncles, and the cousins, to barter, to haggle, and to enjoy the dear delight of bargaining. Now and again the dark funeral cars pass on the way to the cemetery,— a new treatment of an old subject to which one does not easily grow accustomed. A coffin on an open horse-car, with the traditional bravado of the driver thinly diluted to a weak show of respect by a weed on a plug hat; and a more or less indifferent crowd in the covered cars behind, including every grade of grief, from that of simple acquaintance to chief mourner — is worse even than the dreadful funerals at home, with their long string of hired carriages, which yet have some faint semblance of privacy. In strong contrast come the inexpressibly sad burial processions through the country; the coffin borne on the shoulders of friends, and the little handful of sorrowing people walking behind. This has about it the pathos of homely sincerity, that the bathos of vulgar display; and yet one may be as heartfelt as the other.

Along the Viga Canal, leading to the floating gardens, which are now more a name than a reality, the green, slimy water is covered with flat boats and barges, on their way to and from the markets. These are sometimes very beautiful, with masses of vegetables and flowers piled high in fantastic shapes; sometimes as ugly as garbage and offal can make them. Historians of ancient Mexico paint an exquisite picture of the light peroque of the Aztec, floating with the dawn down the shining water toward the Venice-like city on the lake, wreathed in bloom, its flower-crowned crew chanting hymns to the sun god, and the atmosphere of peace and innocence brightening the scene. But time has played havoc with this, as it has with most poetry; and the passage up and down the Viga is very sober prose indeed. Still it is not without interest; and if one's liver is right, and the stomach in perfect order, it is an experience that should by no means be omitted. But do not go with too strong an idea of the Venetian gondola and the gay gondolier.

Although as a rule the exterior is unprepossessing, yet here and there through the city one comes across palaces equally gorgeous inside and out. That of Gonzales, ex-President of the Republic, is of this latter kind. Frescoed on the street fronts in elaborate decoration of red and gold; the finely wrought balconies and screens gilded; the windows glowing with stained glass and carved frames; and the great trellised gates giving glimpses under the archway of a ravishing courtyard, paved in colored marbles, of arbors and Moorish kiosks, of flowers and fountains and gay awnings, — it looks like the pleasure dome of Kubla Khan, the House of Delight of good Haroun Alraschid, the Palace of Pleasure of Prince Fortunatus, or some magical garden stolen bodily from the Arabian Nights, rather than a real home for real every-day living. If the floating rumors of a country mean any thing at all, the retired official who owns it understands financiering to a degree which makes Boss Tweed a bungler, and Eno a child in petticoats. During the few years of his administration, he is credited with personal subsidies on the national treasury, so continued, so enormous, and so splendidly audacious, as to lift them into the region of high art. On the principle that the man who kills another man is called a murderer, while the one who kills ten thousand others becomes a hero, his transactions, which would seem to belong of right to the Newgate Calendar, are considered in the light of diplomatic triumphs; and, to all appearances, his people are proud of his repute. The only difference of opinion we found in his regard was as to whether he had taken out three millions of dollars or twenty-three. If, as is reported, he has built other palaces and other properties as beautiful as this, he has probably done as much good with the money as if it were left to sink in internecine squabbles, or be stolen by other revolutionary communists; and no doubt he salves his battered conscience with this moral reflection. The present incumbent is made of better stuff.

The custom of naming the shops after some fact or fancy has been a constant source of amusement to us all through the country, but it reaches the climax of ludicrous perfection here. It is not altogether new, even at home, to meet a saloon or corner grocery with some such fanciful appellation as "The Arbor," "The Abbey," or "The Golden Lion." But this universal baptism without rhyme or reason, and the utter absurdity to which the limitless tropical imagination has led the sponsors of every business house, from a two-foot-square pulque stand, to a gilded emporium of fashion, would make the framer of the Connecticut Blue Laws laugh out in meeting-time. "The Fountain of Love," "The Triumph of Dynamite," "The Flight of Time," "The Tempest of the Soul," are some of those I find in my note-book, taken indiscriminately along the street. "The Tail of the Devil" and "The Little Hell" might have been placed over their respective liquor counters by a temperance lecturer looking toward the eternal fitness of things; but would he consent to "The Spirit of Purity" and "The Balm of Sorrow," over two similar grog-shops a little farther on?

CHAPTER V

ON THE SOUTHERN SLOPE

PASSING away from the city on the way to Toluca, a landscape of enchanting loveliness, with some new features both in vegetation and architecture, unfolds itself. The mesquite takes the shape of our apple-trees, only with a more delicious green; the vegetable gardens are as delicate and fresh as flower patches; the houses look like Swiss chalets, or the huts built along the Norwegian Alps, with broad overhanging roofs held down by great stones. The hills become remarkably steep; and the sudden downdropped valleys stretch their cultivated fields to the very summits. The poorest house has its plat of flowers, and cage or two of mocking-birds, at the door. Most exquisite views open at each new curve of the climbing road; grand as those of Colorado, but with a picturesque entourage that gives a subtle foreign aroma which that wild beauty lacks. Hills, mountain-sides, deep cup-like valleys, all are glowing with verdure; and the loving touch of humanity softens the rugged grandeur of Nature. The odd, pretty, miserable houses, with walls of adobe, and roof of thatch or fluted scales of red tiles; the lofty, deep-domed sky, clear and dazzling; the clouds resting ever on far-off mountain-tops; the marshy meadows, with innumerable herds of cattle and swarthy shepherds standing knee-deep in the water, are another and a newer page of fascination. Wild, rocky gorges open sometimes suddenly at the road-side; abrupt cañons drop between the hills; deep chasms and sheer precipices leap to unknown depths; but always beyond, the peaceful valleys smile, and the blue mountains keep guard against sense of strife or danger. Wretchedly poor as its inhabitants seem to be, there are compensations. Ignorant of care, untroubled by longing, untortured by ambition, their lot may have more of blessing than we imagine.

On the crest of one hill we looked down a deep ravine to the City of Mexico, thirty-two hundred feet below, and forty miles away. An ocean of overlapping mountains, tossed together like wind-swept billows, surrounded a nest of small valleys, that dimpled in a thousand forms of picturesque beauty as far as the eye could reach. Divided only by brilliant green hedges of the maguey, the climbing fields of rich brown soil, fresh ploughed for tillage, crept to the topmost point of the nearer heights; a rapid mountain stream, fringed with drooping willows, crossed here and there by rude bridges, ran through the centre, and fell like an arrow of light into the depths below. A steep mountain-path, up which a train of burros were painfully climbing, passed over the crest of the nearest hill to some farther valley beyond. The pink towers of an old church, half hidden in trees, rose in bold relief on the summit of one hill; on the slope of another, a ranche of adobe, with dull red roof, made a glorious bit of color; and over the most distant peak of all, the dense shadow of a departing thunder-cloud was smitten by one strong beam of brilliant sunshine, which broke, like Ithuriel's spear, into a thousand sparkling points below.

Now and again a whirling sandspout rose in an airy column, far off on some gray desert-like plain, as we passed. A motionless fisher with his net, standing in a shallow pool, rested like a fine statue-like figure against the sky; the drooping scarlet flowers of a wilderness of pepper-trees stretched away on either side; and far on the hillside, a silent village, its pale clay walls shining behind adobe hedges, lifted its ruined church-tower amid a sombre grove of cypress. Enormous heaps of corn-stalks for fodder, and grain gathered into piles as large as a New-England barn, showed how the resources of the country are being husbanded to prevent a repetition of the famine which devasted its homes a few years ago. Still farther on begins the winding, limpid river, which runs between its high clay banks, down the different terraces of table-lands in this lovely region, and makes the valley of Toluca, with its two or three crops a year, one of the most fertile and valuable in all Mexico.

At Flor de Maria, on the shady side of the station platform, we found the most primitive form of industry we had yet encountered. Indian women were spinning yarn from the wool of the black sheep of that region, by means of a short wooden rod like a thick knitting-needle, with a little button slipped above the tip to keep the thread from sliding off. One pointed tip rested in a small gourd placed upon the ground, and the stick was made to revolve upon this by a swift whirling motion of the fingers. The left hand, meantime, drew the long soft strips of carded wool with a slow movement, into a sufficient tenuity to allow of its being twisted in a strong but rough yarn, around the twirling impromptu spinning-wheel. The rapidity with which the thread gathered upon the reel seemed little short of miraculous, in view of the very original method used in producing it. We bought one of the primitive implements for twenty-five cents. But when we desired to add a yard of narrow cloth woven from the same thread upon a hand loom, the weaver demanded the goodly sum of eight dollars; which shows, if it shows any thing, that even the untutored child of the Mexican plains, as well as the pampered product of nineteenth-century civilization, knows the difference between the manufactured article and the raw material.

One who travels by rail the descending slope from the capital toward Vera Cruz passes in a few hours through all the gradations of altitude which required days to scale on the other side.

This entails some altogether novel experiences. At Esperanza, in the early dawn, one leaves frost by the roadside, and a bracing air blown from the snowy brow of Orizaba, seven miles distant. A little tract of country outside the town reminds one of New England in June, but instantly the glimpse of home vanishes. At El Boca del Monte, or "The Mouth of the Mountain," after passing for some time through a rocky gorge, the train emerges upon what we would call a trestle-bridge, but which has been christened by these imaginative people in a phrase which explains itself, — El Balcon del Diabolo. The steeply sloping mountain-side leaps at one swift bound into the valley of La Joya, the Gem, three thousand feet below. A miracle of loveliness, full of deep, verdant beauty; its rich fields stretching far up the precipitous sides of the opposite heights, with the tiny village of Maltrata, a mass of softly tinted walls and tiled roofs gathered around the spire of the parish church, — it glows like a jewel in the sunshine. Down the spurs of the hills, cataracts of stunted pines and grizzly cactus-bushes sweep like dark avalanches, broken in their course by splintered rocks; and Orizaba, a fillet of white cloud bound beneath its shining brow, fills the eastern sky with glory. Every moment of descent changes the scene. Now it is a deep ravine sweeping downward a thousand feet, filled with pine and oak, mesquite and pepper trees; now a sudden leap into space, as if the solid earth had lapsed beneath one's feet and left one suspended in air, so slight is the frail supporting trestle-work; now a rocky, cloven gorge sweeping to dizzy heights and depths, while the crawling train clings to its rugged side like a fly creeping across a church wall. New kinds of vegetation bloom in clusters of scarlet bells in the crevices, and strange ferns in shaded spots; sparkling mountain water leaps in cascades, or plays hide and seek amid the shrubbery; and the swift-climbing mountains interlace in a network of spurs and slopes, around which the sturdy double-headed engine twists and turns, bounding down a grade that descends three thousand feet in twelve miles. Somewhere, always, the white height of Orizaba crowns the scene; but the curves of the road bring it first on one side, then on the other, until, "And the mountains skipped like lambs" becomes a fact instead of a figure in one's mind.

Down and down we drop to the valley level, and the awful beauty of the descent is marked like a cobweb thread across the mountain-sides. Fields of pale yellow sugar-cane, bound for the harvest, like sheaves of golden spears, occasional clumps of banana-trees, and the deep green of tobacco-leaves begin to alternate with the usual crops. At the pretty station, a crowd of shy women hold up odd woven baskets of straw, filled with oranges, limes, lemons, baked meats, fresh eggs, cakes, dulces, any thing to find a customer. We pass the "Little Hell," a black chasm in which a mad river foams and frets through riven walls, and stop beyond in a paradise of flowers; for this luxurious mode of travelling allows us to stop where we will, for flowers, or sights, or dinner, or hot boxes. By the side of the little stream which runs through the valley, we find maiden-hair ferns, and a wall of small Scotch roses growing like wreaths on tendrils ten feet long; we find gigantic hibiscus like masses of flame and fire, and waxen Yucca lilies, and pale purple bells with the smell of wild violets, and wood-anemones, frail but exquisite. The cars grow drowsy with bloom and fragrance, and we throw the beautiful evanescent things away a few miles beyond, for the pleasure of picking more. It is a feast of flowers. We go on through a series of enchanting valleys, where small cottages, with enormous sloping cone-shaped roofs of thatch, nestle in the midst of lavish beauty, and fields where every product of the temperate zone alternates with every product of the tropics. We pass fields of yellow squash blossoms and tomato plants, of pease, beans, corn, lettuce, and radishes, side by side with mamae and pawpaw, limes and pomegranates. The mountains change from bare summits, stained with rare mineral dyes, to masses of luxuriant green from base to crown; a wealth of rich color and fragrance spreads over field and height; a luscious, rank magnificence of growth, which bewilders while it charms.

And before noontime of that same frosty morning you will probably be walking about a coffee plantation; the beautiful plants or trees, from ten to fifteen feet in height, covered with small, shiny leaves, dark and burnished like holly, with bright red fruit similar to our cranberry both in color and size. All around the garden the long, banner-like leaf of the banana is waving above great clusters of fruit. The air is heavy with odors of orange-blossoms, shining like waxen stars through glossy green leaves, by the side of glowing golden fruit. Immense pineapples are ripening within whorls of spear-like foliage, with a rich musky fragrance. The peasant huts, with conical thatched roofs reaching nearly to the ground, are half hidden in luxurious masses of unknown but beautiful bushes; and the large sculptured leaves of the palmetto emphasize the strangeness that surrounds you. If you are fortunate as we, you will find an olive-skinned group under the overhanging veranda of the overseer's house; the children swinging in palm-leaf hammocks; the withered grandmother crooning to a baby, on the corner of the wide wooden bench; and the graceful matron ready to draw a gourd full of fresh water for you from the scriptural-looking well under the tamarind-tree. In her long white robe, loosely gathered about the waist by a sash, great rings in her small ears, and a triple necklace falling down on the dusky bosom, she was not unlike Rebecca. The whole atmosphere was redolent of a world new, strange, and untried; and the Mexico we had learned to know looked strangely familiar compared with this one. The heat was something terrific, as if it smouldered in silent intensity; the castor-plants, grown to large trees, with long spikes of blossoms and pendant sheaths of berries, looked as if they needed no further refinement of furnace to reduce them to oil; yet the laborers worked on, in sun or shade, as the case might be, as if a temperature of a hundred and twenty-five degrees was a normal condition.

The fervor and glow of this tropical country is incredible to one who has never experienced it. Earth seems to have revelled in a thousand fantastic forms of frolic life in mere wantonness. Every hair's-breadth of soil is covered with a tangle of rare and strange forms; interlacing vines leap from tree to tree, and luxuriant parasites cling to the boughs as if jealous of filling every open space. Lavish blossoms, in gorgeous masses of red and yellow, glow alike on tree and shrub, until one almost fancies the forests filled with the gaudy plumage of birds, so large and striking are the separate blossoms. Here and there, as in the falls of the Atoyac, the water breaks through some mountain-gap, to bury itself in a fathomless depth of verdure below, and a rich, sensuous delight holds one enthralled in a delicious languor.

It is paradise for the body, but it is too much for the soul. Spiritual strength weakens before this luxurious mass of material force. I cannot conceive of great work being done in this seductive world. Beautiful as Circe, it is the mortal, and not the immortal, to whom its fascinations appeal.

This memorable day, which began at a temperature of thirty-two degrees, and climaxed at noon with a white heat of ninety-seven degrees in the shade; with its unequalled experience of temperate zones and tropic; with its gallery of pictures, which stamped themselves like instantaneous photographs on tenacious memory, — was made more memorable yet by the most wonderful succession of cloud effects about Orizaba in the early eventide. While the valley through which we were passing was dark with night shadows, the dome-like summit, radiant with crimson sunset-glow, lifted its glorious, shining head into the pure, pale air, while a dense mass of cloud swept between it and the lordly base, lost already in the growing darkness. It transcended all we had yet known of mountain scenery, and its nearness made the towering height stupendous.

We stopped at length on the brink of a precipice on the summit of the hills, in a white radiance of moonlight that made the world almost unearthly. The snow-covered dome of the mountain looked as if bathed in molten silver; faint home-lights glanced here and there, like fire-flies, from the obscure depths of the valley, three thousand feet below; a long, wavering line of forest fires ran like a glowing red snake up the opposite hillside. On the back platform of the rear car, the dark-eyed Spanish conductor sang Castilian love-songs and Italian airs to the accompaniment of his guitar; and, as the full, liquid tones rolled out upon the night, the doors of wayside cabins opened softly, and groups of silent, dark-eyed Indians gathered near to listen. The people seem to love music as they love flowers and birds, intuitively; and we were not surprised to learn that a conservatory for the education of promising voices was established in Mexico. The perfect simplicity and kindness with which this handsome young fellow entertained us through the long midsummer evening could only be possible in a country like this; and it was as charming as it was new in conductors.

On the journey toward Vera Cruz, the traveller,

entering from the north, is brought for the first time into close contact with those immense plantations of the maguey, which form one of the largest industries of the country at present. Here for hundreds of miles the plains and hillsides are covered with long, close lines of agave in every stage, from the strong, large, generous beauty of the full-grown plant, to the small, tender green of the newly transplanted shoots. If one can conceive the symmetry of these regular forms, with the spiked, fleshy leaves, eight or ten feet long, falling in a whorl around the central blossom-stalk with the regularity of sculpture, and conceive also the effect of seeing them spread over such vast tracts of country, he will have before him one of the most novel pictures in this land of novelty. The plant is to the native what the cocoa-palm is to the South-Sea Islander; it combines within itself a dozen different materials for comfort and use. Growing on an absolutely dry soil, with no help from irrigation, it has a property of condensing moisture and coolness about its roots, which makes it yield at full growth an incredible amount of liquid. The difficulty of finding certain information regarding any thing here, where the usual answer to inquiry is a shrug and a "Quien sabe?" has kept us from finding definitely the facts regarding pulque-making up to the present time. The plant, after from six to eight years' growth, develops in the centre a large circular cone, which, if allowed to increase, would become a thick stalk, bearing the blossom atop. The cone being removed at this early stage, leaves a deep, bowl-like hollow, into which the juice pours at the rate of four to six quarts daily for two or three months. The slightly acrid fluid is drawn off by means of rude siphons, and left from ten to fourteen days in enormous vats, covered inside with hides, the hairy side out, for some chemical reason. A slight froth rises during the process of fermentation, which is skimmed off; and the pulque is drawn into casks or pig-skins ready for transportation. What attraction to taste, sight, or smell this thin, sticky, sour, pale beverage can have, is one of the mysteries a stranger can never hope to elucidate. Still, as nearly every luxury in every land is an acquired taste, from the decayed fish and birdsnest of the Chinese, to the Roquefort cheese and olive of Western civilization, we ought not to quarrel with this manifestation. Throughout the length and breadth of this country, the slimy, yeasty, sorrowful stuff has an enthusiastic success.

With this common drink, which is to the Mexican what beer is to the German, or light wine to the Frenchman, the maguey furnishes two others, not unlike our brandy and whiskey, very intoxicating, but, thank goodness! very little used. We saw but two drunken men during our entire journey. It supplies the natives, besides, with a primitive needle and thread, by tearing off one of the sharp spikes and a long thread of fibre; it gives a species of hempen cloth from the coarser tissue, and of paper from the fine inner pulp; it provides a good thatch for houses; and the *débris*, dried, makes fuel in regions where wood is scarce. So that it fills every want, like a general utility man in a small theatre company, and brings its owner a good income besides. It is hard for one to see where the profit comes, when a glass of pulque can be sold so cheaply; but they say that each plant brings an average of about fifty dollars for its six or eight years of life, and its hundred square feet or so of ground room. New cuttings are immediately planted in the places of the exhausted crop, so that a regular rotation of harvests is insured.

On the same southern route is Puebla, the second largest city of the republic, — beautiful, with airy, wholesome streets, and clean, fine houses; with a wilderness of old churches, rich in bronzes, tapestries, and valuable pictures; with fine façades glittering in blue and yellow tiles, and a forest of spires and towers in every soft tint under the sun, purple, pink, amber, and azure. We found new products in the market-places; queer mats of pineapple and maguey fibre, pottery decorated in bold relief, brooms and sombreros, and onyx worked into a thousand ornamental shapes. And presiding over a tawny heap of oranges and a fragrant mass of pineapples, we found the Queen of Sheba, her great eyes shining under a broad straw hat, her plump, dusky shoulders rising from the richly embroidered recesses of her white *camisa,* her bare, small feet and ankles showing under the short scarlet skirt with its barbaric trimming, and a soft, floating sash of vivid colors loosely knotted about her supple waist. She was walking, with a superb step, through the shadows of the arched *portales* as I first saw her, and her gait revealed the goddess. I am sorry to say she was walking toward a pulque counter, and that she tossed off a pint tumbler full with as much *sang-froid* as you would show in taking a glass of ice-water. But she did it with so airy a grace, and with an abandon so different from the usual timid aspect of her sex, that it was irresistible.

The people were better dressed here, the serapes finer, the sandals more like proper foot-coverings, than in any place we had so far reached. There were fewer of the very poor, fewer cripples and beggars and unemployed, than even in the City of Mexico; consequently the general air of content and happiness was greater. The churches offered an embarrassment of riches, and both public buildings and plazas were exceptionally well kept. Its cleanliness was marked, and a corresponding degree of healthfulness made it doubly attractive. At the Hotel de Diligencias, where we had our second purely Mexican dinner, the tables were laid under the arches of the upper gallery of the inner court, under hanging baskets of flowers, with climbing vines and strange shrubs rising from pots of deep blue pottery placed closely around the light balustrade which separated us from the open air. The deep sky, with an occasional fleecy cloud rolling across it, looked down upon us; the deep go,den sunshine broke through the delicate green hedge behind us; strange birds in odd wicker cages answered each other in bursts of melody; it was as lovely a decoration as art could conceive. We had a spicy, hot soup, of flavor unknown to us; omelette, with green herbs; rice, with tomato and red peppers; beef *à la mode;* oyster patties; curry of chicken; jellies, delicate and deliciously moulded; fruits, coffee, cakes, and tea. From the promenade on the flat roof above, we could look down into the court and the pretty impromptu dining-room, like some strange foreign picture. And we could look at something better still, — at the two mysterious and beautiful creatures rising into the serene sky only twenty miles away. Lightly veiled by a transparent silver cloud, which wound about them in a thousand graceful forms, while exquisite lights and shadows stained their rifted sides with deep amethyst and royal purples worthy the mantle of a king, — Ixtaccihuatl and Popocatapetl, brought startlingly near from our change of position, looked down upon us through all the changing hours of one memorable day. Far away on the other side, like a pale shadow, the beautiful peak of Orizaba showed upon the horizon; and fainter yet, the outline of Malinche made itself visible beyond.

It is impossible yet to reconcile the personal dirt of the lower classes, which is indisputable, with the cleanliness of their clothes. Few, even of the poorest, but have a very respectable whiteness in their cotton shirts and drawers; and the towels and napkins, which they use abundantly about their baskets of cakes and dulces, are as snowy as laundry work can make them. They are, besides, beautifully embroidered with the exquisite fine drawn-work for which the women of Mexico are celebrated. It was astonishing to see the beauty and value which had often been added to coarse or common material in this way. The bodices and short-sleeved chemises of the young girls, and even the woollen petticoats of the Indians, were almost invariably ornamented, either in colors or in white. The ease and accuracy with which intricate designs were conceived, or followed from some minute strips of pattern, were astonishing. The recent "crazes" of civilization for art needlework have shown nothing more delicate or more refined than the specimens of work to be seen everywhere here from the hands of the common people. The celebrated embroideries of Fayal look coarse and mechanical in comparison; as soon as their worth is understood by strangers, there will certainly be a legitimate and profitable occupation opened to the women of the country. Much of the skill shown is no doubt due to the teaching of the convent schools, which have always been famous for their training in fine needlework. The gentleness and extreme patience of the popular character lend themselves with especial adaptability to the care required in such manipulation; and the renown which has followed the lace-makers of Belgium may be repeated again for the beautiful work of their southern sisters.

We have been more surprised throughout at the neatness in the country than at the filth. It is easy to see where carelessness creeps in, when water can only be dipped by the saucerful from the narrow trough of a fountain in the smaller towns, or at best be carried in jars from the aqueducts. But it is harder to explain the clean-swept streets and floors, the clean-washed garments, when one reflects that nine times out of ten the one suit, noonday and night, forms the entire stock of wearing apparel, and that cleaning it means the temporary retirement of the family, either publicly or privately. Judging from the number of primitive bathing and washing establishments we met by country brooks and city ditches, wherein father, mother, children, and clothes were all being cleaned together, I am inclined to think they prefer the public demonstration. And why should they not, if it be simpler and easier? Is it their dovelike innocence that is to be condemned, or our prudish wisdom?

CHAPTER VI

SHRINES AND PILGRIMAGES

THERE is something at once inspiring and dreadful in the intensity with which these men work. Where or how the fallacy concerning their laziness has gained ground, it is hard to understand. Whatever they do is done as if salvation depended upon it, and the exertion demanded where manual labor takes the place of steam or horse power is so bitterly hard that it makes their continuous application the more wonderful. We have yet to see the first instance of shirking or of carelessness. Slight of frame, small in stature, with every appearance of delicacy in physique, they will take upon the shoulders as much as five or six men can lift, and carry it an indefinite distance. Under these immense burdens, they trot instead of walking. To see a *mozo* climbing five or six flights of stairs, and traversing acres of corridors, at this swift pace, with a heavy Saratoga trunk on his back; or to meet four laborers rushing through the city streets with a Chickering piano on their shoulders, is a sight to which we are becoming so well used that familiarity robs it of its first painfulness. These brave workers are so surprised and unprepared for either pity or sympathy that we begin to cover both with the negative quality of indifference. Still, to look day after day at street pavers and sweepers, working as if fame or fortune depended on despatch; porters hurrying under the weight of their enormous burdens; farm laborers ploughing, reaping, gathering wood, drawing water, hour after hour, without a turn of the head or lifting of an eyelash for the world outside, decidedly upsets one's preconceived notions, and leaves one in a maze of reflections. This utter absorption of self in his occupation gives a certain dignity to the man; and one finds here often, amid the most menial surroundings, something of that fine spirit — that in-breathing of purpose into action — that makes Millett's Sower a heroic figure. Think of the men lifted above these by every accident of education and fortune, whom we so often see in the fair fields at home, listless, uninterested, careful only to fill the time of their contract; and these earnest, eager, constant laborers become superb.

The miraculous shrine of Our Lady of Guadalupe, six miles outside the City of Mexico, is of great interest, as every spot must be around which centres the hint of spiritual manifestations. This is no place to venture a single comment upon the truth or superstition of the claims made by friends and enemies. To the people of the country it is a real and abiding evidence of the personal intervention of the Divinity in human affairs, and a closer link between the seen and the unseen world. Deluded they may be, and ignorant and absurd; but can a land that believes in spiritualism and faith-cures afford to laugh at them? Are not the crutches and staffs, the votive tablets, and touching simple offerings hung within the silver railing of the shrine at Guadalupe at least as worthy of respectful attention as the voluntary letters and paid advertisements which attest the miracle cures of a more matter-of-fact civilization? "People who live in glass houses should never throw stones;" and I am tired of listening to the audible sneers at so-called

Catholic superstition, when we preserve in our midst to-day a score of myths and delusions equally as vague and less dignified.

From the height upon which the upper chapel is perched, which is reached by such interminable flights of stone steps! a lovely view of the valley of Mexico, only less beautiful than that of Chapultepec, is obtained. The shrunken outline of Lake Texcoco, in the midst of its carbonate plains, shows more clearly than from the other eminence; and piles of shining white chemical matter, like that of the alkali fields of Nevada, glisten in the sun, waiting refining in the reduction works beyond. One understands from this outlook the enormous change that must have taken place in the natural aspect of this vicinity since Cortés and his warlike band crossed the narrow causeway that formed the only communication between the mainland and the city built in the lake, and only a few elevated points like this of Guadalupe lifted themselves above the shining waste of water which stretched for ten miles about. The present condition makes the question of drainage for Mexico a most complex problem. Its surroundings to-day make it not unlike a vast sewer, made possible to live in,

A PICTURE OF THE HOLY FAMILY

or rather not to die in, by the wonderful air and sunshine, and the purity of atmosphere caused by great elevation. Coming from the north, the smooth tablelands rise by such gentle gradations, that one is not conscious of being lifted above the sea-level; but the eight thousand feet are actually there to separate one from the lower world, and bear him into at least comparative security. If it were not for this blessed altitude, and the purity which belongs to it, the city would be a simple death-trap. As it is, matters are bad enough.

It was on the road to Guadalupe that we once saw a picture, which has since become common, but which looked then like a scriptural illustration made real. A young woman, decently and simply dressed, with a sleeping infant in her arms, sitting upon a small, patient burro, passed down a dusty lane under the shadow of a hedge of yuccas, which looked not unlike the Eastern palm. Her long, blue reboso was wound modestly about the head, and covered the form of the little child, whom she was regarding as fondly as the most tender mother could desire. By her side walked, bare-headed for the time being, a handsome, middle-aged man, with a magnificent shock of coal-black hair, and a full, waving beard. A long staff in his hand, and a dull red zarape wound about the body, he looked as much like St. Joseph in the pictures of the Holy Family and the Flight into Egypt as if some artist had assisted at his reproduction. It was a living tableau. We have seen many similar ones since.

As the time comes for leaving this lovely country, its attractions increase, and its discomforts diminish in geometrical progression. The dust, the smells, the heat, the fatigue — what are they now, compared with the full measure of delight which memory has heaped with treasures? What, indeed, have they ever been but passing hinderances, interfering no more with the ultimate sum of happiness, than the fluttering of a swallow's wing breaks the beauty of his swift flight? These two months, taken from the dreariest portion of the Christian year, from sleet and snow and marrow-chilling winds, and given up to *largesse* of sunshine and flowers, to the superb abundance of a richer summer than we had ever dreamed of before, are something to have lived for. So many unnoted strange excellences clamor now for mention before this most inadequate record closes, that one scarce knows where to begin, — the faint, spicy smell of cedar-wood which perfumes the warm air through the entire kingdom; the twitter of small bird voices, sweeter but not so loud as our sparrows at home, in the dawning; the lifting of palm branches knotted with clusters of scarlet poppies in the nave of the great cathedral on Palm Sunday, as the priest's hands were uplifted, in blessed remembrance of the entrance of Christ into Jerusalem; the novelty of waking morning after morning to the delicious certainty of bright skies and warm air, as if some clear-eyed, silver-tongued angel were calling the weather record, instead of the tricksy sprite that presides over New England. And yet I am more convinced than ever of the superiority of our own climate, impish as it often is, for all purposes of progress and advancement. Weak human nature needs the impulse of re-action: it needs sting of cold to spur toward effort. The warm kisses of this southern air would relax the energy of Alaric the Goth. You might transplant a model Vermont household, where the mother rises before dawn, and has hot doughnuts every morning for breakfast; where the children dress by candlelight, and do their chores like clockwork; where the father works like an automaton from cockcrow to dusk, without taking time to eat, preferring wicked dyspepsia to unholy leisure,— you might transplant a colony of these just but sad souls, and in one generation they would be reclining in hammocks, looking at the world through great, contented sleepy eyes, and overpowered by the exertion of clapping their hands in order to call *mozo* or maid to their side with chocolate and cigarettes. The mother might not smoke, but her daughters probably would. The sharp voices would have lowered three full tones, and fallen into a tender minor key; the swift jerkiness of motion would have subsided to a languid, swaying glide; and the whole family would have succumbed to the inertia of this luxurious atmosphere. For, unhappily, laws of nature are stronger than laws of grace; and the law of climatic limitations is strongest of all.

One of the last days we passed in the City of Mexico we had ridden out by Tacubuya to see one of the cemeteries, surrounded by the high walls and stern gates which enclose those silent resting-places throughout the country. Strangely enough, these are always called Pantheons, perhaps with some reverent idea that all who enter within this temple are gods, since they have put on immortality. As we turned into the lovely Paseo, a thunder-cloud which had swept down into the valley lifted enough to show the pale white peaks, while its ragged edges still trailed across the plain. Over the city a hand's-breadth of blue sky shone on a bit of water near it with a cold, steely sparkle; while the soft, hazy darkness still enveloped the mass of trees and buildings beyond. The beautiful stone arches of the aqueducts, bringing water from the hills, shone in the half light with a dignity even greater than that added by radiant sunlight; and the small white villages, each an indistinct mass of walls and towers, nestled into the background of mountains, vague yet beautiful, as adding human interest to the distant scene. Elegance and wealth crowded the long avenue with loveliness and life, poverty and rags crouched by the wayside; and it seemed a type of the country, beautiful, but gloomy; strong with contrasts of light and shadow; rich in plenitude of resources, but poor in opportunities of utilizing them; at once picturesque and pathetic.

The great improvement which statistics show to have taken place since the advent of railroads, and in direct proportion to their use, is one of the most encourageing signs of the times. Already the states have grown to see the enormity of placing barriers between their own free intercourse; and the law has thrown down the petty system of customs which prevailed on each boundary line, as well as the differences in currency which made a cent taken at Zacatecas useless in Querétaro. A common coinage and common laws are to be put in operation throughout the republic. Equally blind is the present system of duties between it and our own country, placing an insurmountable obstacle between free interchange of products and manufactures, and shutting two great nations out of mutual advantages. On our side especially there would be every thing to gain, and nothing to lose, by abolishing the protective tariff. Business is conducted now upon a most unhealthy basis. Credits of a year are given with interest of at least one per cent a month meantime; an unfair taxation makes landed property and incomes free, and leaves the entire burden to fall on the already overladen shoulders of the poor man; and the national school system, which would naturally, by education, open the eyes of the people to these absurdities, is made available by only ten per cent of the population. The railroad has already accomplished much to secure permanence of government, and protection for business ventures, by breaking up the organized bands of robbers which infested some of the richest districts; by bringing newer and more wholesome customs into the slovenly ways of trade; and by minimizing the opportunities for revolt and revolution, which used constantly to threaten permanence of government, by bringing all parts of the country into close and swift connection with the heads of departments at the capital. The next ten years will do wonders to help progress and utilize resources; but, alas! it will change the beautiful, picturesque, unpractical world we have rejoiced in. There is no rose without its thorn.

You will be tempted to think, when you return to El Paso, that you have gotten hold of a very thorny rose indeed, by the time the conscientious officials have turned your trunks upside down, and upset your bundles on the station platform, in search of contraband goods; that is, unless you travel as we did, in a party, and under such honorable auspices that they take your honesty for granted, and pass your luggage untouched. The enormous rate of duty charged between this country and Mexico is something stupendous. Naturally, in a strange land, one likes to pick up here and there some memento of the new people, some trifles of dress or adorning, to make large the wondering eyes of the little tribe at home, and dissipate a little of the obscurity hanging about this far-away world. You gather a penny bit of pottery here, and a shilling vase there. You negotiate for a zarape at Leon, and a pair of coarse leather sandals at Zacatecas. You buy a broken idol at Cholula, a reboso at Silao, a basket at Guanajuato, an onyx paper-weight at Puebla, a handful of opals at Querétaro. And, of course, you get a Guadalahara water-jar, some Aguas Calientes feather-work, a cotton image at Chihuahua, a Guadalupe duck, and a living, breathing, delicious Mexican mocking-bird. Thus much, at least; with probably some of the very cheap trifles which belong distinctively to each little town; so that in the end you have a practical exposition of Mexican life, which is excessively small, entirely valueless except after a sentimental fashion, but intensely satisfactory to yourself. Then your mind begins to be harrowed by dark hints about duties, and whispered suspicions about right of search. Stories are told of this one who had to leave his goods in bond, and that one who had to forfeit them altogether. At last you are confronted by a formidable legal document, as vague and stilted as legal documents always are, which demands in the usual solemn and priggish manner to know whether you declare on oath that you have or haven't such or such manufactures of wool, etc., subject to such and such laws and by-laws. Being a woman, you treat this with the contempt it deserves, and cut the Gordian knot by declining to read it at all. Likewise, being a woman, you are a consistent and conservative free trader (unless your husband happen to be a manufacturer), and you would scorn to yield your principles to any such base persuasion. Shall you, forsooth, strike your colors because there are some paltry odds and ends in your trunk in danger of confiscation? The spirit which animated the Revolutionary heroes animates you.

That the tyrants in this case are of your own race, makes it but the more harrowing. If they can be mean enough, or absurd enough, with their nonsense about protection and tariff, to hunt through all your possessions, and pick out your armful of poor, dear, pretty things, why let them. *You*, at least, will not help them to make out the list. If they take them, they shall do so without leave or license. And so, having seized the bull by the horns, you wait to see whether it is going to toss, or leave you alone. In our case it proved to be the mildest-mannered animal possible; we entered into our kingdom again as untouched by scathe of customs-man or duty as we left it; and so home, without trial or tribulation.

I wonder, if we ever are happy enough to go to Mexico again, whether the long brown fields, with their tufts of strong green grass, will stretch away to the brilliant mountains in the distance; and here and there a water-course gather about it its small oasis of beauty, with the great unsheltered cornbins looking like high-peaked Arab tents on the horizon; whether the picturesque shepherds with their long wands will guide their wandering flocks of sheep and goats across the brown

THE VALLEY OF THE NAME OF GOD 131

desert slopes, and the veiled women will gather about the great gray stone fountains, dipping their red jars full from the shallow water within. I wonder whether the clatter of the tinkling church-bells will steal across the land from softly tinted towers; and reptile forests of cactus snare the sun in shining, prickly leaf and glowing blossom; and hundreds of miles away, past walled town and domed city, the shining peaks of the old volcanoes lift themselves into the bright air against the glowing sky of dawn or sunset. And places like this little valley of Nombre de Dios, which we are passing to-day, lying under the mountains by the river-side, its poor cottagers riding home on tired horses to the desolate, small adobe huts, and the evening meal of tortillas, or walking across the pretty fields, husband holding the hand of wife and child, — I wonder whether, with its Name of God changed to the name of some bustling American manufacturer who will develop the silver and copper of its background of mineral hills, its huts replaced by comfortable frame-houses, its scant mesquite fires changed to labor-saving stoves, its rags discarded for decent clothes, and its ruined towers rebuilt into trim steeples, it will be as lovely, as contented, or as happy as it is to-day. May Heaven grant it! and as to this, so to every other spot in Mexico. But how glad one should be to have seen it before improvement stepped in to civilize and spoil! Just as it is, strange mixture of industry and unthrift, of sweetness and impurity, of barrenness and luxurious richness, of poverty and wealth, of repulsiveness and fascination, has the world to-day any thing better to offer than a Mexican holiday?

7

CHAPTER VII

LITERARY MEXICO: A GROUP OF NOVELS

BEFORE leaving that domain of the picturesque to which its natural scenery and poetic expression belong, it may not be out of place to take a passing glance at the lighter literature of Mexico, as represented in the works of its better known novelists. Choosing, then, as specimens, three or four books from the somewhat limited list at the service of the reader, one is first struck by a certain number of general traits which form a foundation for the superstructures of differing styles and authors. There is, to begin with, an almost universal absence of the finer analytic and subjective writing. Character is painted broadly rather than by delicate touches of detail, and the motives of action are only suggested by the accomplishment of the act. There is a tendency towards epigrammatic terseness in sentence and paragraph; and, except in very rare cases, any close study of psychological phenomena in connection with the conduct of personages is left to the reader himself. He may form his own conclusions, or he may read his tale without drawing therefrom any moral. One finds invariably a deep admiration for nature, expressed in delicate word-painting of scenery, and loving reminiscences of favorite spots. The material environment is always luminous and forceful; there can never be any doubt, in this fine glow of local color, as to where the action of the drama is laid. And there is an immense impulse of patriotic spirit which seems, in spite of time and distance, to propel the author toward the days of revolution and struggle for his *mise en scène*. In the twelve novels we have chosen as a basis for observation, eleven are placed, as to time, amid the complications arising from the events of the years between 1860 and 1867. They might all be historic as well as the two which bear this distinctive title. The single exception is a chronicle of life and customs more than a hundred years ago.

For many reasons this exceptional story is of interest. Purporting to be the garrulous narrative of a man drawing near the limit of extreme age, and relating to children and grandchildren the history of his earlier career, it is as remarkable for minuteness of detail, as are its companion volumes for large generalizations. After the fashion of "Gil Blas," it is interspersed with accounts of the adventures of this or that comrade whom chance has brought into contact with the hero. With much less elegance of style than the celebrated story of Le Sage, it more than repairs this shortcoming by the purity of incident and superior moral tone which pervades its many chapters. With utmost exactness it relates the trivial incidents of infancy, childhood, and youth; each passing event is made the subject of a new disquisition. Mistakes of the time regarding the rearing of children, the sending out of the infant to nurse, the relegating of early training to servants and irresponsible persons, the absurd ignorance of the village schoolmaster, all receive their share of castigation. Laxness of discipline in seminary and college, the strange mingling of trivialities and superstitions which finally assumed the place of education, the mis-usages of society which condemned the offspring of well-to-do parents to the temptations of idleness, each has its own long chapter in the nine hundred pages of this interesting but endless volume. Life on the haciendas, with its private bull-ring, and slow recurring village festas; life in the city, its sole idea of amusement centering about the gambling-table, and the disgraceful orgy of the public ball; life in the home, languid, dull, unoccupied by sense of duty beyond the sluggish routine of domestic affairs, or elevation of purpose save the endeavor to uphold traditions of caste at expense of probity and comfort, all these are delineated with affecting realism. Compared with this picture of customs and manners a century ago, the Mexico of to-day is a land of impetuous progress; but, at the same time, one is surprised to find amid the old-fashioned moralizing of the venerable penitent some of the most approved modern ideas concerning social problems. He declaims against round dancing; he scourges the fashion of wearing mourning graded to express the infinitesimal steps in the passage from deep black grief to pale mauve melancholy; he criticises prison discipline as means of reformation; he castigates the misrule and ignorance of ordinary hospital management. And so through a series of homilies upon affairs of Church and State; of groanings over his own wickedness, tempered by mild senile enjoyment of these youthful escapades; of love and marriage; of vivid interjectional description; and of quotations from Livy, from Horace, from Pliny, from Cicero, from Tacitus and Marcus Aurelius, — the old philosopher gossips over infirmities of time, and hope of immortality. He carries minutiæ of detail even beyond the grave, and leaves behind a Latin inscription to adorn his tomb. The photographic minuteness with which life in those earlier days is depicted makes "El Periquillo Sarniento" an admirable yardstick by which to measure reform.

Among more modern stories, "Guadalupe," by Irenio Paz, editor of the daily paper "La Patria," may be taken as a fair example of the popular novel. Señor Paz is a voluminous writer. The series of bulky volumes bearing his name on the titlepage must tantalize his Northern editorial brother with suggestions of possibilities of leisure with which the latter is perforce unacquainted. Fancy the managing head of the "New-York Herald" indulging in literary distractions which should result in a score of books! The style of this author is simple and direct. The characters

are introduced at once in their true colors, with
an amiable frankness which precludes possibility
of mistake. There can be no doubt as to the
identity of polished villain, or poor but virtuous
hero. There is no complication of mixed person-
ality in which good and evil struggle for the
mastery, and sympathy swings like a pendulum
between disgust and admiration. The narrative
moves through quiet regions of commonplace until
some lofty trait or some deep wickedness needs
illustration, when it suddenly bounds into the
mazes of melodrama, and the reader finds himself
tossed upon stormy billows of heroism, passion,
or remorse, as the case may be. In justice, it
must be acknowledged that these transitions are
infrequent; otherwise the sensation would be too
much that of mental seasickness. The quiet,
homely life which "Guadalupe" depicts, speaks
well for the people who furnish such a record;
and the popular taste which accepts such placid
chronicles of gentle love and religiously tempered
hate is, at least, evidence of a purer and more
wholesome temperament than that which subsists
upon the vicious sensationalism of the American
dime-novel or the outrageous vulgarity of "Peck's

Bad Boy." The interpolated heroics are too obviously constructed for effect to be capable of producing any. They are like the crashing and flashing of a stage thunderstorm. One acknowledges their worth as settings, but they would never perturb the spirit nor turn milk sour.

The picture of home-life among the middle classes, as gathered from this and other works of the same author, is sound and healthy. There is deference to parental authority; there are simple amusements, and close guardianship which watches over intercourse between the sexes; there is naïve expression of opinion in matters of faith and philosophy; and, permeating all, the serenity of easy, unhurried existence, which gently bears rich and poor upon its placid surface. Extremely pleasing are these after the turbid and motley variations which are required to spice parallel histories in our own progressive centres. It is food for pride, as well as patriotism, to observe that a commission of importance to *los Estados Unidos*, and a subsequent tour through that region of high civilization, is the reward reserved for the brave young man who has raised himself by his own efforts from poverty to the position of colonel in "the Army of the Republic," — that Mexican Legion of Honor.

The plot of "Guadalupe" is simple in the extreme, and the *dramatis personæ* old friends, in spite of Spanish mantilla and reboso, — the adopted daughter of a pious widow, who loves in silence and secret the artist son of her benefactress; the youth who in turn worships the heartless sister of his false friend; the futile machinations of the latter to move the orphan girl from the path of duty; the triumph of her fervent and lovely spirit, and the foregone conclusion which changes brotherly affection into devotion of the lover. The incidental glimpses are full of local traits: the pompous pride of the newly rich, as opposed to the graceful virtue of the poor household; the quaint worldliness and naïve reflections of the foolish little worldly maid Amelia, and the equally quaint sweetness of the wild-rose Guadalupe, — are all charming. A certain sketchiness leaves an after-effect of having been introduced to silhouettes, rather than solid figures; still the sense of vagueness only helps that of pleasure. The atmosphere is pure, if not bracing. The heroine reminds one somewhat of Octave Feuillet's "Sybilla;" but she lacks that breath of life which stirs in the veins, and animates the action, of the beloved French girl. Nor has the Mexican author more than a hint of the exquisiteness and *verve* of the Frenchman. He has, however, the cleverness to win popularity, and each of his twenty books runs through two to five editions.

Vicente Riva Palacio, who holds a first place by the elegance and purity of his language, has been also a prolific writer. His prose is imbued with the spirit of poetry. Many of his paragraphs are full of delicate imagery and rhythmic force; with the essence, but without the material form, of the poem. Yet, in an even more marked degree than those of Paz, his books present to a stranger a startling combination of diverse traits. To a loving and tender sympathy with nature, which overflows in descriptive passages of great beauty, and to a spirit of gentle revery, developed with genuine delicacy through a thousand light touches, he adds at times an almost rabid exuberance of melodramatic intensity. These baleful and lurid periods are in strange antithesis to his limpid and earnest utterances. They are like an alarm-fire kindled upon a quiet hillside on a peaceful summer evening. In his "Calvario y Tabor" the reminiscences of the suffering of the people through the years of struggle which culminated in the overthrow of foreign intervention, and the fall of Maximilian, are given with a clear directness that forces them upon the consciousness of the reader as realities. But to this heroic portrayal of suffering and misfortune he attaches so many impossible episodes, and such a climax of romantic and unreal horrors, that the genuine emotion aroused by the simplicity of truth and the touching events of history is in danger of being lost in repulsion. There is something so incongruous in this combination, which can trace the most refined and wholesome impressions, and an imagination which can conceive and revel in a delirium of horrors, that the result is a series of shocks. To a foreigner, at least, it is like touching the two poles of a battery at irregular intervals. The current of admiration and sympathy is being constantly broken up, and as constantly renewed. In the seven hundred pages of this particular book there is a climax of death-scenes which are veritable nightmares. Foreseeing that a certain number of dangerous and unnecessary personages must be gotten rid of, one stands appalled at the ingenuity displayed in making the first taking off so circumstantially terrible. But the author's power is equal to the strain. With magnificent audacity he proceeds and runs through a rising scale of accident, suicide, and murder, which swells on triumphantly to the perfect artistic end. Yet this is but one view of the picture. Side by side with this dark and tragic story moves the peaceful and tender tale of village life and quiet homes and humble affection. It is as if the same hand could write at the same time "Monte Cristo" and the "Vicar of Wakefield," and the frenzied outbursts of the one revenge themselves for the gentle serenity of the other.

"Calvario y Tabor," as the name implies, is a story of suffering and triumph, — the death-agony of the old empire, and the transfiguration of the new republic. With the vivid and thrilling record of sacrifice and heroism, which forces the reader into profound sympathy with the purpose of the people, are interwoven two love-stories, — one dark with passion and intrigue, the other as touching and gentle as the soft beauty of the sylvan landscape in which it is set. Here is the opening note of the pastoral symphony. The scene is laid in the *tierra caliente* on the shore of the Pacific.

"It was an evening in January; and the sun, slowly sinking behind the immense mass of waters, shone like a globe of burning gold through the luminous haze which filled the atmosphere with glory. It appeared to float upon the surface of the waves, which, lifted in long, swelling billows on the high seas, broke in undulations on the sand, bearing into shore curving ripples of shining foam, white as the petals of a lily and brilliant as the stars in the sky of the tropics. Along the banks of a small inlet, running deep into the land, the night air gently bent the graceful crowns of palm-trees, and the feather-like leaves swayed gently over their reflections in the tranquil water beneath, broken by the slow ripples into a thousand mirrored splinters of flower and foliage. From time to time the sinister form of a crocodile glided slowly by, without disturbing the silence. At the entrance to the wood, where the little strand lost itself in a soft carpet of moss, a few huts built of branches, and thatched with leaves, showed through the deeper shadow. Farther back slender columns of smoke, outlined against the paling sky, showed the vicinity of an Indian village; and a murmur of voices, mingled with snatches of song and tinkle of music, blended confusedly, like the notes of a wind-harp.

"By the seaside all the world sings. The deep undertone of the waves fills in the background of harmony. It is impossible to listen to its ceaseless pulsation without feeling the desire to mingle one's voice with the concert which immensity eternally offers to God. The breaking of the billows against the rocks, the lisping of the ripples against the beach, weave the strands of melody; and the soul, by them moved to remembrance, falls into reveries of the past which are either prayers or aspirations, which are like the memory of the lullabies of our mother over the child at her breast, or the lingering notes of the favorite air of the woman one first loved.

"As if in unison with this universal impulse

towards harmony, a young girl of fifteen years emerged, singing, from one of the wood-paths, and turned in the direction of a spring of pure water which bubbled up from a tangle of shrubbery beyond. She was a slight and graceful brunette, wearing the common dress of the women of the coast; her great eyes, dark and brilliant, shone under long, curving lashes; her white teeth and small red lips made enchanting contrast with the pale olive of her cheek; and in the perfect oval of her face was that blended expression of purity and sensitiveness which marks the temperament of a painter or a poet. A loose white camisa, covered with the delicate embroidery in which the gentler sex delight to satisfy their love of adornment, and a simple blue petticoat, formed her attire. But around her throat hung necklaces of gold and coral, on her arms were bracelets of shells and pearls, and her slender fingers bore a profusion of glittering rings. She was doubtless the daughter of a rich house; but among this simple people every woman works, and she bore upon her head one of the huge water-jars of the country, balanced without aid from her hands, and without impairing the dignity and elegance of her carriage. An artist looking upon her might have imagined a new Rebecca; for nothing is more faithful to the biblical idea than the young girls of the coast who come to the wells for water, poising their great red jars upon the head without disturbing in the least their lightness or freedom of motion."

Thus Alejandra, the beautiful brown girl of Acapulco, enters upon the scene of her future trials and triumphs. The idyllic story of homely country life, wherein rich differs from poor only in that the bounty of one supplies the need of the other; the benignant village *padre* and his almost puritanic sister; the loves of Alejandra and Jorge; and the family of strolling players, poor and despised, but happy in virtue, — make a story full of refined sentiment in the midst of the most sensational and forbidding realism. One is introduced to the intimate habits of the people; to the hospitality which makes every house an inn for the stranger; to the charity which adopts the orphan, comforts the unfortunate, and looks upon the idiot as "beloved of God." But there is at the same time an awful picture of corrupt law, distorted justice, and almost absolute want of fixed principle in the government of society.

The historical portion of the novel is superb. We who profess admiration for the qualities of valor and perseverance, who consider ourselves allied in bonds of brotherhood with the oppressed of every land, should be ashamed of our ignorance in regard to the Mexican struggle for independence. The vicissitudes of our own Revolution are tame, the sufferings even of the winter at Valley Forge sink into insignificance, compared with the events of 1864 and 1865, in this tragedy of dolor and endurance. Whole towns were swept out of existence. The population, flying through night and storm, sought asylum in unbroken forests, filled with wild beasts and noxious reptiles, or amid the rocks and caves of desert places. "Ashes marked the location of homes; the direction of roads was outlined by corpses." Menaced by hunger and thirst, decimated by pestilence, the small and lessening band of Republicans melted like smoke before the advancing Imperialists, whose conquering forces carried all before them. Buffeted by every rudeness of fortune, they still persevered in the unequal struggle, and snatched victory at last from the very jaws of death. Like eagles who build their nests upon inaccessible peaks, "the apostles of liberty fled to the mountain tops, to fight and to wait; and too often upon the summits these martyrs found their Calvary." Sometimes, impelled by a sudden fury of passion, a band of devoted men crept down from their fastnesses, cut their way through the midst of the enemy, and perished to a man, joyful in the destruction they dealt in dying. Without money, without clothes, without other arms than the guns in their hands, they fell by the roadside in forced marches, tortured by fatigue and famine, "and were left unburied, for beasts of the field and birds of the air. . . . If a laurel or a palm had been planted to commemorate the memory of each of these, the land would be one impenetrable jungle from end to end." Still they continued on, "a new man stepping into the place of the comrade who had dropped before him, hurrying to new strife, to new sacrifice, in order to convince Napoleon and Maximilian, France and the world, that a people who could so struggle for independence was a people invincible and worthy of being free."

The book, as one might expect from the reputation of its author, is full of fine, sonorous Spanish, glowing with descriptive eloquence and declamatory force.

"Liberty is like the sun. Its first rays are for the mountains; its dying splendor falls likewise upon them. No cry for freedom has first arisen from the plains, as in no landscape is the valley illumined before the heights which surround it. The remnant of the defenders of a free people flies ever to the crags and hills for final security, as the last light of the sun lingers upon the summits when the lowlands are veiled in obscurity." "Never were there heard, after these annihilating combats, the groans and cries of the wounded, which so often find a place in descriptions of deserted battle-fields. Our soldiers suffered and died without appeals for aid or lamentation over life; as heroes expire, valiant and resigned." " Toward the east, only a labyrinth of mountains, which, arid and desolate, lost themselves in the distance; infinite in form, suggesting inexpressible and awful contortions; full of deep, sad shadows, lonely, terrifying, like a sombre and tempestuous ocean, suddenly petrified with awe at the whisper of God." "Nations, like Christ, have their Tabor and Calvary. Only, while the Son of God passed first to transfiguration and thence to the cross, it is the contrary with them. For nations are composed of mortals; the Spirit of God can alone support the sorrow of Calvary after the glory of Tabor." "Our wars have been like the bloody but beneficent operations of the surgeon, who amputates the gangrenous member through kindness to the sufferer; not like the wounds given by an assassin, who seeks to destroy his victim. Europe condemns without understanding us; America understands without condemning, but she remains silent. God, history, and the future will acknowledge our purpose and our triumph."

Ignacio Manuel Altamirano is equally well known as orator and author. His "Paisajes y Leyendes," records of the customs and traditions of Mexico, is as marked for its temperate and even style as Palacio's work for vehemence and contrast. Confining himself principally to the religious festivals of the country, with their earlier as well as later observances, he gives us charming pictures of the fervor of a primitive race, carrying into their observance of Christian rites many suggestions of the more innocent forms of their old worship. He is evidently as widely read in the modern classics as El Periquillo Sarniento was in the ancient. French, English, German — all literatures have laid their flowers at his feet, and his versatile fancy culls from each in turn to adorn his page. But it is when he relies upon himself that he is most attractive. The legend of "Our Lord of the Holy Mountain" is enriched by a sketch of the holy friar, Father Martin de Valencia, of whom it is recorded, that "every morning, as he went out of his cave, after passing the night in prayer and meditation, the little birds did gather in the trees above his head, making gracious harmony, and helping in praise of the Creator. And as he moved from place to place, the birds did follow; nor, since his death, have any been ever seen there."

Reminiscences of the author's boyhood in the little city of Tixtla, with the entire population following the procession of Corpus Christi through streets arched with green boughs, and garlanded with blossoms, remind one of the Passion Play of Oberammergau. Such ardor of devotion, such reverent silence, such echo of sweetness from the low-chanting Indian choristers, flower-crowned, and bearing branches of new-budded orchard trees, in order that their fruits might find favor in the eyes of God, form an ideal picture of religious enthusiasm. It reads like a sketch of the Middle Ages. So does the description of the houses, decorated with every treasured atom of color and drapery; and the generalissimo marching at the head with his band of native troops. So, too, does the story of Holy Week, beginning before dawn on Palm Sunday with young men and maidens scouring fields and woods for the first wild-flowers, with which to decorate their palm-branches. The account of the lifting up of these palms, braided and knotted with flowers, during the canon of the mass, corresponds precisely with what we saw in the Cathedral of Mexico last year.

Juan Mateos is famous not only at home, but abroad. He has reached the point at which a man becomes a prophet in his own country. His brother authors quote him as they would Goethe or Lord Byron. His novels are mainly historical. The style irresistibly recalls the elder Dumas;

even the look of the page has that abrupt brevity of sentence which is so characteristic of the French novelist. In "El Cerro de las Campanas" he gives intense and dramatic expression again to the story of the "Usurpation." With only a thread of narrative to sustain interest, he places before us a careful *résumé* of the "episode of Maximilian." It is pleasant to note, that, in spite of evident and deep sympathy with the republic and the leaders of the people, he speaks of the hapless emperor more with sorrow than anger, and gives a touching pathos to the death-scene on the lonely "Hill of the Bells," which has so often moved the sympathy of strangers. His hatred and scorn are reserved for the Cæsar of the Tuileries, "who sacrificed on the altar of ambition an unfortunate and lovely princess, as well as the young Archduke of Austria, whose ensanguined corpse cries yet for vengeance from the imperial tomb at Vienna, wherein it waits the vivifying breath of the resurrection." Dramatist as well as artist, his actors naturally group themselves upon the stage of history or fiction; and each succession of scenes culminates in a *tableau.* The rush and power of his expression sweep one most eloquently toward the author's conclusions.

In outward appearance, the Mexican novel is exceedingly unattractive. Like the French and German *brochure*, it is usually unbound; like many of our own, it is printed in poor type, on miserable paper. It has ragged edges; and it stretches beyond any normal limit, reaching from seven hundred to a thousand pages in almost every case. The books are evidently not intended for summer reading, nor for a people living on the high-pressure principle that obtains in America, which makes the incessant and furious activity of the steam-engine the highest example for human imitation. When illustrated, the cuts are so poor, and of such ludicrous horror, that they would turn the deepest sentiment into ridicule. Above all, they are enormously dear. Such a scale of prices would not be possible in a country which counted a large number of readers of fiction among its population. With the appetite for such intellectual refection comes a garnishing of the dish in which it is served, as well as a cheapening of the cost of refreshment. I am not altogether sure but that the demand for these books, although so small in proportion to the number of individuals, does not show a higher degree of appreciation than our omnivorous devouring of odds and ends. When, in despite of coarse texture, rude letterpress, very low art, and very high prices, a book runs through six or eight editions, it is reasonable to suppose some higher motive in its perusal than the criminal one of killing time. And in the face of melodramatic tendency, and archaic mixture of sentiment and commonplace; in the face of incoherence of action, and want of subtle analytic power; yet with its deference to the ideal of womanhood, its large love of nature, its tribute to the home virtues, its loyalty to national traits, its admiration for simplicity and purity of character, and its enthusiastic patriotism,—the Mexican novel would seem to have found this more elevated plain, and based upon it a recognized right to existence.

The list of Mexican authors stretches almost indefinitely. Besides those already mentioned as novelists, Manuel Payno, Pedro Castera, Peon Contreras, Vicente Morales, and José Maria Esteva are well known as brilliant and forcible writers. Upon more serious topics, whether of political or social importance, one finds the names of Zarco, Prieto, Baranda, Siliceo, Arriaga, Ocampo, Alcaráz, Lerdo, Montes, Zamacono, Yañes, Mariscal, and many others, who have contributed largely to the education of the people. As poets, a still greater number of popular and celebrated men and women find honorable place in the ranks. Guillermo Prieto is probably best known in what might be called national songs, full of originality and patriotism. José Maria Esteva follows him closely in giving expression to the natural traits and habits of the country. Acuña, Luis G. Ortiz, Silva, Gutierrez-Najera, Dias-Miron, Covarrubias, Juan Valle, Eduardo Zárate, Francisco Colina, Firso de Córdova, Apapite Silva, Manuel Romero, Esther Fapia, Rosa Carreto, Refugio Argumeda de Ortiz, and Miguel Ulloa. Justo Sierra, one of the most virile and forceful singers, and Manuel Flores, by his tenderness and sweetness, have taken high rank among Spanish poets, even outside their own country. In view of the impression which is now gaining ground among literary people, that the writing of poetry is the best school for the formation of purity of style in prose, it may be interesting to note that almost every popular Mexican romancist is also a popular poet. Among famous religious writers are Sister Juana de la Cruz, Señor Carpio-Pesado, Arango, Bishop Montesdeoca, and others. As dramatists, Gorostiza and Alarcon rank well among Spanish classics; while Calderon, Rodriguez-Galvan, Chavero, Mateos, Contreras, Acuña, and others have produced much skilful and remarkable work. Señors Juan de Dios, Pesa, and De las Rosas hold an enviable place as poets of the home and domestic life. As linguists, Señors Altamirano, Yscalbalceta, and Pimentel are best known, the latter having made important studies upon the Indian dialects of the country; while Orozco y Berra, in his "History of Ancient Mexico," has excelled all previous writers upon the same subject. The best author upon constitutional subjects, or those relating to political economy, is probably Señor Vallarta ; but each of these lists of authors could be re-enforced by numberless names. These given are, perhaps, enough to disabuse the American mind of any feeling that Mexico lacks the expression of literary tastes, or suffers in comparison with other lands from want of scholarly interpretation.

CHAPTER VIII

BLOSSOMS OF VERSE

SINCE poetry is the flower of sentiment, and its highest expression of beauty and fragrance, one may be pardoned for closing this very inadequate sketch of picturesque Mexico by a word in its regard. Upon reflection it should not appear strange that a country in which the fiery imagination of the Castilian had been grafted upon the native gentleness of the Aztec, should blossom into verse as naturally as a plant turns toward the light. The love of flowers and birds, which is indigenous here, is always closely allied to that of song, in the heart of a nation; so that one should not be unprepared to find evidence of very general poetic feeling in a race which both history and tradition have dowered with exceptional qualities of sweetness and tenderness, and which since the Conquest has had its native predilections trained into higher literary art by education and association. Yet it is a pleasant surprise to one unfamiliar with modern authorship in Mexico to find the Muse so entirely at home, as the little volume, from which the subsequent translations are taken, would indicate. Under any circumstances, a book containing upon its titlepage the names of fifty poets "of reputation and popularity" might be considered worthy attention, even without a preface apologizing for the ungraciousness of being obliged to choose so few among the ranks of representative writers. A country which can count its native poets in such wholesale numbers would certainly seem to have more than its average share.

The plan of the work is unique. Eighty or ninety pen pictures of Mexican women of position, distinguished among their associates for beauty, for talent, or for the higher grace of fascination, form its contents. A prologue, which might better be called a rhapsody, vindicates its motive. "Never has the loveliness or the virtue of woman shone more resplendently than when lifted upon the wings of poetry into the realms of the ideal; as when proclaimed in rhythmic cadence by the lyre of the poet, whose sensitive and passionate soul is alone capable of comprehending her. Her beauty, her tenderness, her smiles, her tears, have been the inspiration of the names that live through ages. It was she who made immortal Dante and Petrarch, Goethe and Alfred de Musset. It is for want of her inspiration that we doubt the right of Cervantes to be called a poet, in spite of his genius, and deny that of Castelar, in spite of his artistic talent. The latter contracted a civil marriage with History and Politics. From this literary polygamy may spring such daughters as Fame, as Glory, even as Immortality, but never one whose name is Poetry. . . . To sing the praise of that being, as delicate as beautiful, as loving as resigned, as generous as tender, as modest as heroic; of her who is all love and sacrifice, who has come into the world to be the beloved companion of youth, and the sweet consoler of age; who gives wisdom to science, genius to art, and heroes to the native land,—ah, to sing of woman is for the poet to pay the divine debt of inspiration to the highest work of humanity, and to the being who has brought divinity down to earth!"

The verses that follow are in no sense love-songs. There is scarce a tinge of passion or a hint of the glowing sensuousness of tropical imagination in the entire book. Indeed, it errs somewhat in the other extreme. Its expression is based upon the colder and more formal models of the early English and French writers, with a certain stateliness of diction and fondness for mythological simile which belonged to the conception of poetry two centuries ago. But the verse remains, in this case, almost wholly uninformed by that enthusiastic flame of devotion, which often, in old times, rendered the transparent disguise of stilted phraseology incapable of hiding the natural glow within.

The idea of prefixing to each little poem the full name of its subject has a piquancy altogether Southern. We would choose, under similar circumstances, to shoot our arrows of song in the dark, or at best against a shadowy target of initials, leaving our reader to discover their aim, — half annoyed if he should guess rightly, wholly angry if he went astray. These more sincere, or perhaps more artful, people go straight to the mark. The friend or admirer chants his hymn of praise under his lady's lattice and in the open light of day. If this be too unreserved for love,

A POETIC EPIGRAM 163

it is likewise too personal for friendship. One can judge of the absolute result better by listening to the strain.

The chief value of the book lies without doubt in the insight it gives concerning a phase of Mexican character little credited by the outside world, — the appreciation of woman. The preface might be quoted entire, for the elevation of its sentiment and the purity of its ideal of the sex. Space allows us to choose only one of its lighter and more graceful thoughts, interpolated in the prose text to give the editor's conception of the theme which inspired the volume:—

> "'And what is Poesy?' she said,
>   As laughingly she questioned me.
> 'The smile upon thy lips; the red,
> Ripe bloom upon thy cheek so fair;
> The glinting of thy golden hair;
> Those flashing eyes that scorn control;
> Thy budding form; thy waking soul—
>   Thou, thou thyself art Poesy!'"

The first number is dedicated to Carmen Romero Rubio de Diaz, wife of the president. It is in a more hackneyed vein, and neither so graceful nor so expressive as many of the others. We may charitably suppose that the exalted rank of the first lady in the land somewhat overshadowed the genius of the writer, or that its insertion was an after-thought suggested by policy, and that desire to curry favor in high places, from which, alas! even poets are not wholly exempt. This is the more to be regretted, since the dark, bright beauty of Señora Diaz ought to be a prolific source of inspiration to the fortunate mortal who chose it as a text. The best lines are in this simile: —

> "Generous as the stream that spreads
> Its rich gifts 'mid garden-beds,
> Yet alike through weed and sand
> Flows in blessing through the land."

The translations following are taken entirely at random, and given as literally as diverse rhythms, impossible in English, will permit. I notice in particular one oddity of construction which seems to mark a favorite form. The lines, regular in rhyme and length, begin with a small letter; but occasionally, at spasmodic intervals, and without any connection with the grammatical division of sentences, a capital is prefixed: —

A PORTRAIT

"TO JOSEPHINA ESPERON.

"From her red lips' chalice fair
Flower-like perfume fills the air;
And her voice, like song of bird,
Thrills the heart at every word.
In her eyes' dark light divine
Glories born of sunset shine,
And in radiant splendor preach
Eloquence that passeth speech.

If her beauty could but stand
Mirrored by an artist's hand,
Or inspire a poet's theme,
Men would think it but a dream."

The subject of the next bit of verse has inscribed an odd mixture of sentiment and materialism in her interpreter. The combination of the earthly music-teacher with the many heavenly benefactors of the beautiful singer is a triumph of realism. In the original, the abrupt transition is even more marked, since the line rendered, "The muse who presides," etc., is written, —

"El gran Melesio
En el Conservatorio," —

a much more mythical personage to the world at large than the one by whom I have replaced him.

"TO VIRGINIA CARRASQUEDO.

"Not hers are her graces;
To gods they belong!
From Venus her charms;
Love lent her his arms;
The Muse who presides
Over harmony's tides
Hath shared with her gladly the sceptre of song!

Morales, the master,
Doth list and rejoice.
Says: 'More than Ulysses'
My fear and my bliss is:
He heard but the ringing
Of sirens' sweet singing;
I know the full charm of Virginia's voice.'"

A particularly graceful expression runs through the next lines:—

"TO VALENTINA GOMEZ FARIAS.

"If he should chant thy wondrous grace,
Dumb would the singer's music be;
If he should strive to picture thee,
Never a line could artist trace.
For of a soul so pure as thine,
How could the semblance e'er be true,
If the glad brush that painted you
Had not been dipped in tints divine,
Or if the poet's lyre had known
No tones save those of earth alone!"

Many of the lines are brightened by *jeux d'esprit*, depending for point upon Spanish words in which similarity of sound or spelling covers a totally different meaning. The archness of the little verse which follows is more comprehensible and decidedly epigrammatic : —

"TO GUADALUPE DE LA FUENTE.

"Once Cupid's eyes were clear,
  Open, and kind;
But, alas! *you*, my dear,
  He chanced to find;
Only one glance he gave, —
Since then, who paints the knave
  Must paint him blind."

Concha is at once the name of a sea-shell, and the pretty Spanish diminutive of the name Concepcion. In sober prose it would be questionable whether a pearl was ever found in any thing more romantic than an oyster-shell. But who would be such an iconoclast as to overthrow a poetic image for the forlorn comfort of setting up in its place a paltry fact in natural history?

"TO CONCHA MARTINEZ.

" Above the white foam and the azure sea
    A gleaming shell doth float,
And the bright sun that glows resplendently
    Kisseth the fairy boat.

The world it glads with beauty doth not know
    The treasure in its breast, —
The precious pearl, that, radiant as the snow,
    Within its heart doth rest.

Sweet Concha! on life's sea thy beauty rides,
    And man's applause doth win;
But only we who love thee know it hides
    The fair white soul within."

"TO MARIA AMELIA ROMO.

" Earth was a bower of roses rare and pale,
    And heaven a starry sea;
Through the soft shadow sang the nightingale
    His wondrous melody.
'Twas springtime, and the dewy dawn was wet,
    When, from its dreaming stirred,
The flower's soul, in sweetness rising, met
    The bright soul of the bird;
And from that kiss thy loveliness was born,
    Fair shrine that doth enclose
The song-bird's voice, the brightness of the morn,
    The perfume of the rose."

In some cases the tribute is paid in a prose form, or rather in one which suggests the metrical swing and irregular cadence of Walt Whitman. I transcribe literally a portion of one: —

"TO MARIA ALFARO.

"Nature,
Splendid in all her manifestations,
  Has offered the poet
An infinite number of exquisite forms
With which to compare woman.
But the glowing imaginations of these votaries of Apollo
Not content with the enchanting realities
Of flowers, of stars, of sunbeams, of birds,
Of palm-trees, of pearls, of diamonds —
Have flown from the visible world
To seek the forms of seraphs and angels,
  Of celestial powers,
And of the marvellous visions with which fancy has peopled
    infinite space,
To discover new graces
With which to adorn their idol.

Amid this wealth of brilliant and magnificent images,
From this universe of real or imaginary beauties,
I, who have now reached in my wandering the frigid and narrow
    zone of old age,
Desire to choose from my remembrances
A flower, a pearl, a star,

Which may serve as an emblem of a young girl
Who has flashed
Across these later days of my life.
Is she a jasmine, blossom sister of the violet,
And, like it, hiding
From profane gaze of the vulgar?
Is she Modesty, insensible to the allurements of flattery?
Is she the spirit of cheerfulness?
Is she angel of the fireside?
Is she sunshine?
Is she perfume?
Alas, I know not!
In vain I question my soul;
Neither in one image
Nor in all,
Can I find the counterpart of Maria Alfaro."

I close with an occasional stanza or two from longer poems: —

"TO MARIA AUBERT Y DUPONT.

"If, mid the shades on high,
   They should meet, nor know her name,
   'Beatrice!' would Dante exclaim,
'Leonora!' would Tasso sigh."

"TO ROSARIO [1] BARREDA.

"Many a beautiful brown girl, splendid,
   With eyes of the night and morning blended,
     Springs from the soil of Vera Cruz;

[1] The same word, "Rosario," is at once the name of a girl and a rosary.

But amid all the loveliest faces,
Show me but one of your height and graces, —
    If but the gods would let me choose!

Exquisite rose of perfection! soon
    You can no longer hide; and then,
When your bright face from the balcony shines,
Under your window will hang, as at shrines,
    Rosaries — made from the hearts of men."

"TO ELENA FUENTES.

"If for beautiful Helen of old,
    Chosen by Paris, a city fell,
And heroes of Greece spent life and gold,
    How many Troys, under Fate's grim spell,
Would perish by fire and sword for thee,
If each one who sees thee might Paris be!"

It will be seen, that, although in these songs there is no very marked degree of originality in thought or sentiment, there is yet a most dexterous handling of the similes which have been used to illustrate woman's loveliness through so many centuries, and an aptness of phrasing which often puts them in a new light. There is, besides, a great cleverness in the use of poetical forms, and evidence of much practical experience in their use, — a good stock of tools, and skilful hands in their management. One may regret the want of that freshness of conception which the mind naturally expects in the productions of a people with whose traditions it is unfamiliar, and whose comparative isolation inspires the hope of individuality. But there is still much to be grateful for. It is doubtful whether a subject so exciting to the imagination, and so opportune for the introduction of warmth and sensuousness of expression, has ever before been treated by a guild of poets with an equal delicacy and purity. And, without claiming any greater credit, I think it must be allowed that the blossoms of this Mexican garden show a higher cultivation and a more refined taste than our ignorance has been led to expect from the every-day products of the Aztec soil; and that for this reason, if for no other, they deserve more than a passing sense of pleasure in their beauty and fragrance.

PART II

POLITICAL AND PROGRESSIVE MEXICO

BY

MARGARET F. SULLIVAN

CHAPTER IX

FROM CONQUEST TO INDEPENDENCE

"THE art and beauty of historical composition," said Capt. Bernal Diaz del Castillo, a lieutenant of Cortez, "is to write the truth;" and from the year of our Lord one thousand five hundred and seventy-two, when, "in the residence of the royal court of audience," the Spanish historian finished his narrative, down to our own days, there has been only one story of the pictorial aspects of Mexico. The vivid and accurate description which is given in these pages is not surpassed for precision, for taste, for sympathy, by that of any earlier writer of all who may say with Mrs. Blake, as Bernal Diaz said of himself, "This is no history of distant nations, nor vain reveries: I relate that of which I was an eye-witness, and not idle reports or hearsay; for truth is sacred."

But whoever undertakes to write of material Mexico, even though he can say with equal truth that he was an eye-witness, and holds truth sacred, will find himself falling into vain revery. "Reports" he may procure, but, in more senses than one, they are "vain;" hearsay he will find copious and contradictory; and although hundreds of authors have travelled the country, and left their impressions on record, out of the mass of their labor little that is of absolute value can be extracted.

Diaz himself complains of the elegance and untrustworthiness of the earlier work of Francisco Lopez de Gomara. The Abbé Clavigero, who wrote of Mexico one hundred and fifty years later, enumerates forty Spanish, Italian, and Mexican historians from whose pages he derived his own narrative; and he alludes somewhat doubtfully to a long catalogue of French, English, Dutch, Flemish, and German writers of whom he is not willing to admit that they held truth sacred. His patience was justly exhausted by one among them who described native princes going on elephants to the court of the Montezumas. One is impressed, however, in reading the literature of the past about this strange and still only dimly understood country, with the permanency of nearly every thing in it. Bernal Diaz himself was not less affected than Mrs. Blake by the wondrous beauty of the landscape; while others, of a later date, have written about the manufactures and customs of the country in phraseology which we, who were there only yesterday, as it seems, would scarcely alter. Don Antonio de Solis, for instance, "secretary and historiographer to his Catholic Majesty," tells us that he saw cotton cloths "well wove, and so fine that they could not be known from silk but by feeling." "A quantity of plumes," he continues, "and other curiosities made of feathers, and whose beauty and natural variety of colors (found on rare birds that country produces) so placed and mixed with wonderful art, distributing the several colors, and shadowing the light with the dark so exactly, that, without making use of artificial colors or of the pencil, they could draw pictures, and would undertake to imitate nature." The same work contains an excellent woodcut of Mexican women making bread. The process, the utensils, the implements, are precisely the same as those which Mrs. Blake describes as now in use.

Writers in the present century only repeat the

narratives of those of the preceding ones. "Notes on Mexico" in 1822, by "A Citizen of the United States," and printed in Philadelphia, might have been written two hundred years ago, or last week. Mexico is in many things the unchanging country of this continent. The American acknowledges his debt to the works of Lorenzana, Alzate, Clavigero, Boturini, Mier, Robinson, and Humboldt; but by far the most interesting portion of his volume is his unadorned tale of what he saw and heard.

The arcades in the neighborhood of the cathedral, in which we spent a good deal of time, existed in his day. "They resemble the bazars of the East, and are furnished with every variety of goods." Costumes have changed no more than the making of intoxicants.

In 1836 Charles Joseph Latrobe wrote "The Rambler in Mexico." If we should take his account of scenes during Lent, it would be unnecessary to alter a word. Mexican piety is somewhat theatrical and realistic during that holy season. On Maunday Thursday, for instance, they fill the air with the cricket-like sound of rattles, made in all manner of designs, of wood or silver, the substitute for bells; and on Good Friday they disport Judases of all shapes and sizes, filled with gunpowder, which at the proper moment explodes. On Palm Sunday they fill the churches in their indescribable variety of gay and striking costumes, bearing in their hands tall, yellow palms, making a much more impressive sight, and closer to the narrative of the Gospels, than our colder climate enables us to have. Capt. G. F. Lyon, who went from England to Mexico in 1828, examined closely the labor, especially the mining, of the country. Herdsmen received five dollars per month, and agricultural laborers seven pence per day. Wages have slightly risen since then, but, unfortunately, so have the prices of food and clothing. "Mexico as it was and is," by Brantz Mayer, was written in 1841–42 by the Secretary of the American Legation. He sought especially to collect data from authentic sources upon commerce, agriculture, manufactures, coinage, mines, church and general government. He is obliged to add: "In many instances I have only been enabled to present estimates." Two recent writers, Thomas A. Janvier[1] and David

[1] The Mexican Guide. By Thomas A. Janvier. Scribners.

A. Wells,[1] have been similarly engaged. They have produced useful, but differing compilations. In many instances they have been able only to present estimates. During our stay in the City of Mexico, we examined all the book-stores, and endeavored to enlist the interest of kind friends there for the procurement of statistical publications upon material Mexico. The result was two books, — one, "Atlas Metodico," by Antonio Garcia Cubas, from the titlepage of which it is apparent that there is a geographical and statistical society; but this atlas contains only local geographical information and maps, with two pages of questions for teachers and students. The other book was "Annuario Universal," editor Philomena Mata, and the issue for 1886 was the eighth annual publication. It is a well-printed duodecimo, two columns to the page, a thousand pages solid nonpareil; and the total of the statistics in it occupies less than four pages. The custom-house claims the rest.

Partly from observation and partly out of authorities selected from various groups, — in an effort to keep clear of partisans against Mexico, —

[1] A Study of Mexico. By David A. Wells, LL.D., D.C.R. Appleton.

and with the understanding that in statistics estimates must be employed often in lieu of ascertained facts, I venture to offer some brief considerations.

"For the commission was to be extended no farther than barter and obtaining gold."
In that sentence, written by Bernal Diaz, is compressed the whole story of the Spanish invasion of Mexico, its scope, its motive, its object. The part that religion played in it is acknowledged by the same unquestionable witness with like candor. When Cortés was ready to set out upon the expedition, he caused to be made a standard of gold and velvet, with the royal arms, and a cross embroidered thereon, and a Latin motto, the meaning of which was, "Brothers, follow this holy cross with true faith, for with it we shall conquer." The occasional words of the Spanish captains to the natives concerning religion appear to have been called forth more by the shock of seeing human sacrifices, and hearing that children's flesh was served upon the table of Montezuma, than by any earnest desire to induce the Mexicans to embrace Christianity.

If they had any such desire, their own conduct was more than sufficient to account for the refusal of Montezuma to act upon their suggestion; and the letters of Cortés himself, as well as the writings of many of his companions and contemporaries, show that what defects the visitor in Mexico may see to-day in the social organization are precisely of the kind of Christianity which the Spaniards taught by their example. The vices their chroniclers denounce in the emperor and native princes on one page, they themselves adopt on the next; and the most revolting practices, abhorrent to faith, and ruinous of the most firmly organized society, find avowals in language intermixed with prayers and ejaculations of devotion. They charge the natives with superstition: they were themselves superstitious. They charge the natives with low morals: they added lower ones, if lower were possible. They charge the natives with cruelty: they set up the Inquisition among them to enable the State to be cruel, while the name of the Church was borrowed to wear the responsibility, and carry down to our own time the reproach.[1] They charge the natives with

[1] Janvier, p. 27.

treachery: they taught them masterly tactics in that vice, when they procured entrance into the palace and confidence of Montezuma.[1]

No matter who, after Cortés, ruled Mexico for Spain, he carried out the original design of the governor of Cuba who planned the invasion. Barter and the obtaining of gold, with the employment of religion as a means to that end, is written over every chapter of Spanish rule; and the traditions of despotism, the bigotry against commerce, the hostility towards foreigners, the avarice and sloth which politicians infused into the religious orders for their own ends, resulting at last in a great crisis, are all directly traceable to the rapacity, the hypocrisy, and the feudalism of the invaders.

It would have made no difference if the invader had been England, and the new religion Protestantism. The Spanish domination in Mexico lasted for just three hundred years, from 1521 to 1821. "The government, or viceroyalty, estab-

[1] Mr. Wells seems a little unfair to the military character of the Mexicans, when he directs attention to the fact that Cortez conquered the empire with so insignificant a force. Treachery on the part of the invaders, and hospitality on that of the natives, had as much as arms to do with his success.

lished by Spain in Mexico seems to have always regarded the attainment of three things or results as the object for which it was mainly constituted, and to have allowed nothing of sentiment or of humanitarian consideration to stand for one moment in the way of their rigorous prosecution and realization. These were, first, to collect and pay into the royal treasury the largest possible amount of annual revenue; second, to extend and magnify the authority and work of the established Church; third, to protect home [i.e. Spanish] industries."[1] Is not that the description of the English domination in Ireland? The consequences are curiously correspondent. The land in Mexico, like the land in Ireland, is owned by a small number of proprietors. The tillers in Mexico have no more interest in the results of their toil, than had the tenants in Ireland prior to the beginning of the land-reform era forced upon the English Government by the people of Ireland. The Mexican landlords reside abroad in large numbers, like the absentee landlords of Ireland; and the money produced by the soil flows out of Mexico in exports of bullion for these absentees and their

[1] David A. Wells.

creditors, precisely as the crops and money of Ireland are carried from her to replenish the purses of her landlords. The native manufactures of Mexico, slight as they were, were discouraged by the Spanish administration, for the same reason that England destroyed the more vigorous industries of Ireland as rapidly as they appeared. Mexico was to buy only from the manufacturers and merchants of Spain; gold and silver, woods, and a few products of soil and labor combined, she was required to give in exchange for what Spain had to sell. Ireland and India have been required to give products of labor and soil combined in exchange for English manufactures. Religion in each case was degraded into the uses of the conqueror. Human greed was the passion in both cases. The sleep of Mexico, disturbed at intervals by hideous convulsions, was the result on this continent. A more muscular race made a more persistent resistance to England, and Ireland has begun the recovery of her complete rights. India's day is not yet at hand.

It is a droll satire upon political economy, that Spain accomplished her purpose by protection in Mexico, and England by free trade in Ireland and

India. There is no abstract theory yet devised by man superior to natural avarice enforced by arms.

A patriot priest, the divine instinct of nationality carrying him above the dreaming masses of his fellow-countrymen, at length arose against the Spanish domination. He paid with his life for his devotion to his country, but the death of Hidalgo blew the breath of liberty into Mexico. His country relapsed for a time under the old oppression. In another decade she made another desperate and more successful, but far from sufficient, effort; and, when the flag of the republic was unfurled in 1821, the symbol upon it was that of the old native race, — the eagle and cactus, the emblems of the Aztecs. A people without means of inter-communication, of different languages, in whom the poetry of paganism was often mingled with a dull understanding of Christian principles; whose more subdued classes scarcely cared to be awakened to exertion, and whose intellectualized caste was filled with languid selfishness; a people who had no interest in their land, no manufactures, no education; whose wants were simple and easily supplied;

who knew little of arms, and possessed none, — it was impossible that such a people should be eager in seizing upon chances for the erection of representative government on the ruins of hereditary despotism; hereditary, that is, not in the line of the Spanish viceroys, but in the ideas by which Mexico was held under foreign rule. It is not wonderful that revolution followed revolution. It is not surprising that province attacked province, and faction collided with faction.

With the expulsion of the Spaniards, new foes came in from without. England, the usurer of the world, advanced money upon what she intended to be, as in the case of Egypt, the security of the entire country. The United States was beguiled into an invasion by which Mexican valor was made to stand a superb test against soldiers, who, unlike Cortés and his companions, defeated the Mexicans by arms, but not by treachery. Not the worst misfortune which befell Mexico in consequence of the Northern invasion was the increase of her obligations to England. A direct consequence of her bankruptcy was the intrigue of France, Spain, and England for the invasion of Mexico after the breaking out of our civil war.

The progress of that struggle convinced two of the copartners that the contemplated enterprise would be perilous, with the Monroe Doctrine still vital, and a considerable army of experienced troops, North and South, to answer with equal alacrity the call of their common country to expel European despotism from this continent. Louis Napoleon, desperate for new delusions to postpone his fall, resolved to take the chances; and the last invasion of Mexico was the child of his ambition.

It is true that Maximilian was not the designer of his own ruin. It is unquestioned that he was anxious to win the good-will of the Mexican people, and that it would have been the highest happiness to him and his amiable wife to have ruled Mexico for her own good. The earth is not yet ready to dispense with the luxuries of royalty, and large aggregations of the human race are persuaded that it is wise to pay for the glitter and mockery of thrones. And it may be true that a monarchy in Mexico, constitutional and conservative, maintained with just firmness, would have afforded that tranquillity essential to national development. But experience, human nature, and the re-consolidation of the United States were all opposed to Maximilian, — experience, because there is no instance of genuine or enduring national development under a ruler representing political and industrial interests opposed to those of the people he tried to rule; human nature, because his own blind and deceitful course rendered it certain that he should fail; and the re-consolidation of the United States, because the spirit of the American people, calm after the conflict, and purged by the effacement of slavery from their own soil, would not suffer Old-World despotism to repeat in our own day the story of earlier ages.

Maximilian, and the still more deeply and deservedly pitied Carlotta, have been the cause of much denunciation of the Mexican people. To refuse sympathy to Louis Napoleon's hapless and beautiful victim, whose reason toppled after her heart was broken, is surely beyond human power. The sternest heart cannot tread unmoved the lonely cypress paths of Chapultepec, where her sad feet sought to escape the troop of sorrows that encompassed her husband. Toussaint l'Ouverture, the emancipator, dragged from his farm in Hayti by the treachery of the great Napoleon, and starved to death in the dungeon of Joux on the bleak and snowy Jura, is the companion picture for the demented daughter of the king of the Belgians, widowed and crazed, in a palace of the Montezumas, by the last of the Napoleons.

Maximilian had the misfortune to follow too closely the example of his patron. His assumption of the crown of Mexico was made contingent upon a popular vote of approval; but the assembly of re-actionaries who went through that ceremony for him no more represented the people of Mexico than the people of any other land. The pretext served its purpose; but he speedily freed himself from those who had been the aiders of his fortunes. The spoliation of the Church by the republic, ruthless and undiscriminating, had created a conservative party, not blameless altogether, but yet honest; and to that party Maximilian was pledged. To that party he owed his crown. He cast them off in the expectation that he could succeed better by making friends of their enemies. At the same time, acting, it is charged, upon the advice of Bazaine, and defying the best sentiment of all classes of the people, defying humanity itself, he issued a decree which would have revolted Cortés himself. He ordered that all persons found in rebellion against his pretensions should be shot as outlaws. This appalling order sealed his own doom. The mercy he showed to Mexico, Mexico showed to him. It was a noble impulse which induced our Government to plead for his life on condition that he should leave the country whose soil, as a pretender to a crown, he had no right to touch. It would have been better heeded had Mexico been able to recall to life those whom, loving their native land, and justified in resisting foreign invasion, he had relentlessly sent to unhonored graves.

Could Mexico have hoped for much under a ruler who sought to force a monarchy upon a people who had heroically established a republic; from a prince whose exemplars were Napoleons; whose first step after his enthronement was the betrayal of those who had enthroned him, whose second was an order for the massacre of political opponents? What is there in the traditions of crowns won by invasion, maintained by treachery, and spattered with popular blood, to justify the expectation that Maximilian would have taught the Mexicans self-government?

The only way for a nation to learn self-government is to practise it.

CHAPTER X

CONSTITUTION AND GOVERNMENT

THE present government reflects in form the progress of all nations, and in spirit the troubled past of Mexico. Its constitution is modelled upon that of the United States, and in its present form was adopted in 1857. All persons born within the republic are free, and, if slaves, become freemen by entering it. Personal liberty, with its full significance, is guaranteed, including liberty of the press, "with this reservation, that private rights and the public peace shall not be violated."[1] The press law, many of whose provisions are admirable, has been administered in a manner to discourage enterprise. There are, we are told, fifteen daily papers in the capital. Only two of them printed news, as we understand the word; but an association was being formed to effect a connection with our press associations

[1] Janvier.

for the procurement of at least a summary of European and the principal American intelligence. Financial reasons, traditions, and custom make news important in Mexico in this order: first, English; second, Spanish and Continental European; lastly, North American. The papers are very partisan, in that respect imitating the press generally of all countries. The "Times" of London, in its "opinions," is no broader than the narrowest faction print of Mexico; and the news upon which its editorial utterances are based, in affairs political and religious, is quite as trustworthy as its opinions are unbiassed. Last summer it printed from Rome a story that the Jesuits had poisoned the Pope, and that they alone possessed the antidote by which his life could be saved. They consented to save it on condition that he should issue an encyclical restoring to the order its full privileges, etc. This romance was printed with perfect soberness in the telegraphic columns; and an editorial, ponderous and a column long, declared that the Jesuits ought not to be blamed, but that the vanity of the pontiff in consenting to save his life at such a price was deplorable. We never saw that matched for fact or philosophy in any publication in Mexico.

The constitution of Mexico recognizes every right recognized by our own organic law. The federal power is vested in three departments, as with us. The legislature consists of two houses. The members of the Chamber of Deputies are elected every two years, one for each forty thousand of the inhabitants. There are two senators for each state, half of them elected every two years. Congress sits from April 1 to May 31, and from Sept. 16 to Dec. 16. The president, whose term is for four years, is aided by a cabinet composed of ministers of foreign affairs, of internal affairs, of justice and instruction, of public works, of finance, of war and marine. The judicial power resides in the supreme court and in the district and circuit courts. Formerly the chief justice succeeded to the executive office in case of the death or disability of the president. Now the succession passes to the president and vice-president of the Senate, and the chairman of the standing committee of Congress, — a small representative body peculiar to the political organization of Mexico. It sits during the recess of the legislature. The justices of the higher courts are elected for a term of six years, and associated with them are an attorney-general and a public prosecutor, similarly selected. The State governments copy the constitution of the federal government so far as their relative position permits. The president is commander-in-chief of the army and navy. The former is composed of three sections, — the active army, nominally sixty-eight thousand men, actually at present less than half that number; the reserve, twenty-four thousand men; and the general reserve, seventy thousand. The cavalry arm is well equipped, and there is a small artillery branch. The national military school at Chapultepec is one of the best institutions of the kind existing, and receives its students after the example of West Point. The navy is limited to three or four small vessels, incapable of other than coast patrol service. The national sentiment which the government seeks to promote is indicated by the national festivals, — Feb. 5, adoption of the federal constitution in 1857; May 5, victory over the French in 1862; May 8, birthday of the patriot priest Hidalgo; May 15, capture of Maximilian in 1867; Sept. 15 and 16, declaration of independence by Hidalgo, 1810.

The area of the country is 778,590 square miles, estimated, for there has never been a complete survey; with a population of ten million, estimated, for there has never been an authentic census. The political divisions are four states on the northern frontier, five on the gulf, seven on the "grande oceano," and eleven in the interior; with one territory, and the federal district corresponding to our District of Columbia, except that the federal district is represented in Congress as a state.

While the form of the government is thus approvable, the spirit of it is represented as more or less despotic. Nor is it clear how it can be otherwise. I found it everywhere asserted that the masses of the people take no interest in politics, and the official vote for president sustains this. Why, then, should not the administration be despotic? The fountain will not rise higher than the source. The people are not homogeneous; their languages serve to keep them from understanding each other; the mutual hostility of Church and State widens the chasm.

Free public assemblies for the discussion of political matters are as yet unknown, and must be impracticable for some time longer. "Public opinion" is the expression of class interest; and "class" means now, in Mexico, the landlords, the professional men, the practical politicians (who are generally old soldiers and young lawyers), the students, and the generals of the armies. We were told, by patriotic persons, that the federal government is so unscrupulously centralizing that it practically controls all the state governments. On the contrary, Mr. Wells came to the conclusion that the state governments are less under federal control than in the United States. This contradictoriness embarrasses the visitor at every turn and in every thing. Many of the most intelligent Mexicans we met expressed poignant regret over the fate of Maximilian and the erection of the republic. We put to two gentlemen of equal intelligence and undoubted candor, but of different pursuits, this question: "Which would the people prefer, the empire or a republic?" They answered simultaneously; but one said the empire, and the other said the republic. Each was confident that the other was mistaken. He who preferred the empire was a German and a manufacturer. The advocate of the republic was a professor of mathematics.

The fact remains, that the republic was born of Mexican ideas, has been maintained exclusively by Mexican arms, is based upon sound principles, and must gradually awaken the entire people into a healthful and independent interest in its perpetuation. Charges of dishonesty are freely made against men in high administrative place, as well as against government officials generally. We had no means of ascertaining how much truth might be in these assertions. If they be true, Mexico cannot be accused of isolation in that, at least. No judgment upon the Government would be reasonable which does not take into account the configuration of the country; its immense foreign debt, for which the present Government should be held not responsible beyond certain moderate limits; the enormous expenditure required, and the inconsiderable revenue obtainable; the sources whence the revenue must for the present be derived; and the social state, due almost entirely to the effects of foreign misrule. "Barter and the obtaining of gold" for Spain has left a stamp upon Mexico which one generation of comparatively tranquil independence cannot be expected to efface. A traveller who passed through the country many years ago saw a face peering out of a window upon a vista of wonderful beauty. Whether prisoner or recluse he knew not, but said through the grating, "How beautiful!" "Transeuntibus," was the laconic answer, — "To those who pass by." So has it been with Mexico. Beautiful to those who robbed her, beautiful to the tourist, her real condition is one which depresses her own people, whose poverty, ignorance, and loneliness make them the most pitiable, as they are certainly the most kindly and polite, people on this continent.

CHAPTER XI

RELIGION AND EDUCATION

IF we look more closely at the Mexico of this century, of this quarter of the century, and of the present decade, it becomes apparent that a change, organic and constitutional, has been silently coming upon this ancient and secluded country. It is not a change brought about by war, nor substantially advanced by diplomacy. It is a silent revolution, moving gently in the footsteps of peace. We must seek the evidences of it in education, agriculture, and manufactures, and in the sources and uses of revenue.

The story of education in Mexico is one of hopelessly tangled threads. As the mystic symbols on the monuments of Egypt have only begun to yield their secrets to the archæologist, we need not despair of yet knowing something of the antiquity of a country whose age is beyond present estimate, and whose earliest civilization, as indicated by her superstitions, architecture, costumes, and myths, was Oriental. Of her middle age, that long period following the Spanish invasion, and preceding authentic accessible accounts by travellers or natives, the vain spirit of exaggeration has been the chief exploring activity. On the one hand, hostile prejudice has charged against the ostensible religion of the Spaniards the results due in large measure to natural causes, which neither political forms nor moral forces could easily overcome. On the other, shallow religious partisanship has credited the Spaniards with achievements in Mexico, educational and moral, of which there is little material proof.

Itemizers of history, for instance, who rush into discussion with an isolated date, and who assume the dignity of the architect with the function of the brick-carrier, have made ado over the fact that the first university on this continent was established in Mexico in 1551. It is not true even as an isolated fact. If it were true, its historical value would consist in the impression it made on the national life, not in its categorical precedence. The ceremonious authority for the creation of a university in Mexico was given by

Charles V. of Spain in that year; but the actual beginning was not made until two years later, and then in temporary buildings. The institution could not have known a prosperous infancy, for it had no home -of its own for nearly another half-century. The building which now bears its name was not put up for nearly two centuries later. Very little trustworthy information can be procured concerning its founders. It was a child of Salamanca, and Salamanca in the middle of the sixteenth century was in its glory as the exponent and defender of Thomas Aquinas. His latest biographer, speaking of the Christian Fathers, says, "They did not veil themselves away from the sight of men when they took up their pens to write; but on the contrary, with beautiful frankness and simplicity, they wove their own portraits in amongst their teachings, and that with a grace and an unconsciousness of self which are amongst the most charming characteristics of single-minded genius."[1] The pioneers of Christian learning in Mexico did not follow their example, but nevertheless they were brave and devoted, as well as erudite and pious,

[1] Saint Thomas of Aquin. By the Very Rev. Roger Bede Vaughan.

as is manifest from their abandonment of their native land and the intellectual luxuries of its university society, for the hardships, mental and physical, of a land to be reached by perils of a still strange sea.

Doubtless the university of Mexico did something for science and art; but its usefulness was necessarily restricted to those who learned or inherited the Spanish tongue, and were able to acquire the preparatory education requisite for admission. That the area of its usefulness was very narrow, needs no demonstration. It must have had some independence and aggressive energy, for it was several times suppressed by the Spanish Government. In 1822 a visitor found the building very spacious, and the institution well endowed; "but at present there are very few students." Two hundred is the highest number mentioned as having been in attendance at any time. The library consisted then "of a small collection of books." In the city there were "a few book-shops," and the few books in them "were extravagantly dear."[1] "Under the colonial

---

[1] The book-stores are not numerous now; but books, and uncommon ones, are cheap. I found in a second-hand shop Tom Moore's Odes of

system liberal studies were discouraged." In 1844, when Brantz Mayer was in the capital, the appropriation for the salaries of the professors in the university was $7,613. There was no appropriation for elementary schools. Of the colleges he says, "The students who live within the walls are expected to contribute for their education, while others, who only attend the lectures of the professors, are exempt from all costs and charges; so that about two-thirds of the pupils of every college receive their literary education gratuitously." Colleges appear to have been then as useless as the university; for out of a population of seven millions, less than seven hundred thousand could read.

In a well-known Church history published in 1878, it is said, "There is but one university in the country, that of the City of Mexico, founded in 1551, having twenty-two professors and a library of fifty thousand volumes."[1] The statement,

---

Anacreon (1802); Aventuras de Gil Blas, 4 vols., Barcelona, 1817; Thesaurus Hispano-Latinus, Madrid, 1794; La Gerusalemme Liberata, Turin, 1830; El Nuevo Testamento, London, 1874. The imprimatur is that of the Cardinal Archbishop of Westminster. The volume contains an excellent map and many good illustrations. The translation is approved by the Archbishop of Santiago.

[1] Alzog: Universal Church History.

whether it refers to the year of the foundation or the year of the publication, is certainly misleading. The reference is probably to the year of publication, but it must have been based on much earlier records; for there is no university in the country to-day, and there was none in 1878. It was abolished in 1865. The building was first transferred to the Ministry of Public Works; now it is the National Conservatory of Music. Among the subjects of the paintings in the interior are St. Thomas, St. Paul, St. Catherine, and Duns Scotus.

The charge that the Spaniards endeavored to prevent the spread of letters, and that the Church has antagonized education, requires careful examination. The printing-press was set up twenty years after the conquest. The natives could be reached by the press only through the extension of the Spanish language. The Spaniards, unlike the English in Ireland, did not make the native tongue penal, and enact special statutes for hanging, disembowelling, exiling, or imprisoning those who employed it for teaching purposes. They kept the printing-press busy turning out dictionaries, by which rulers and ruled were enabled to get a little nearer each other. They printed books of devotion, — a fact which irritates some; but would they have had the Greek classics printed for the natives, and works on metaphysics, science, and natural philosophy? Who could have read them? It is true that the printing-press does not seem to have accomplished much. But the obstacles in its way were like their enormous mountain-ranges, which kept forever apart, unless they met in war, tribes, if not races, whose dialects were inexchangeable. The printing-press had to make, not one Spanish-Indian or Aztec dictionary, but as many dictionaries as there were tongues. The natives refused the Spanish spelling-book, and continued to hate and tease the invaders. To-day this diversity of speech remains to prove that the failure of the printing-press does not constitute good ground for indictment. There are at least five distinct languages in Mexico, and millions of the people remain totally or partially ignorant of the official language of the republic.

There was, moreover, a political force always at work against the diffusion of education through the agencies of the Church. It was the same cause which operated in Ireland : the Church, maintained by the State, was not maintained for the sake of religion or education, but to provide for favored sons of the invaders. The bishoprics were filled with appointees of the Spanish court. The support of their establishments was made a legal burden, and the story of the Established Church in Mexico runs in a parallel with that of the Established Church in Ireland. "It was the policy of the Spanish cabinet to cherish the temporalities of the Mexican Church. The rights of primogeniture forced the younger sons either into the profession of arms or of religion, and it was requisite that ample provision should be made for them in secure and splendid establishments. Thus all the lucrative and easy benefices came into the hands of Spaniards or their descendants, and by far the greater portion of the more elevated ecclesiastics were persons of high birth or influential connections."[1] It was inevitable that the causes and customs which gave princely incomes to clergymen without congregations in Ireland; which enabled bishops of the Establishment, entering as paupers their sparse dioceses, to leave

[1] Brantz Mayer.

legacies of thousands of pounds to their personal heirs, while thousands from whom their tithes were wrung died unlettered and in want, — should create in Mexico an ecclesiastical class and condition of a corresponding kind. "As long as Mexico was a dependency of Spain, . . . the bishops had very handsome revenues; the largest being about a hundred and thirty thousand dollars, and the smallest about twenty-five thousand dollars."[1] The real estate and personal property of the religious establishments accumulated, from an estimate of ninety million dollars in 1844, until, when the revolution arrived, the material wealth of the Church furnished temptations too great to be resisted.

As late as 1829 the Spanish court disputed with the Pope the right to nominate bishops for Mexico. In that year there was only one see filled in the entire country. The rival parties of the country made the most of the political factiousness which surrounded religious office; and in 1833 it was proposed to confiscate the Church property, and apply the proceeds to the payment of the national debt. This was slowly and spas-

[1] Brantz Mayer.

modically done, and was fully accomplished when Maximilian arrived in the capital as emperor. Alzog relates the rest of the chapter: "Directly on his arrival . . . the clerical party demanded the immediate and unconditional restoration of the ecclesiastical property confiscated and sold during the ascendency of Juarez and the French agency. As this amounted to about one-third of the real estate of the empire, and one-half of the immovable property of the municipalities, and had already passed from the first to the second, and in some instances to the third, purchaser, it was plainly impossible for the emperor to satisfy this demand." The papal nuncio avowed his inability to find any satisfactory solution of the question, and resigned. Maximilian instructed his ministers to bring in a bill, which was promptly passed, vesting the management and sale of ecclesiastical property in the council of state.

What Brantz Mayer wrote of the common clergy in 1844 doubtless continued to be true: " Throughout the republic no persons have been more universally the agents of charity, and the ministers of mercy, than the rural clergy. The village *curas* are the advisers, the friends, and protectors of their flocks. Their houses have been the hospitable retreats of every traveller. Upon all occasions they constituted themselves the defenders of the Indians, and contributed toward the maintenance of institutions of benevolence. They have interposed in all attempts at persecution, and, wherever the people were menaced with injustice, stood forth the champions of their outraged rights. To this class, however, the wealth of the Church was of small import." That is the testimony of an enemy of the Church. It is corroborated by that most imposing fact in Mexican history since the invasion, — that it was a priest who led the people in their first genuine effort to throw off a foreign yoke, and found a national republican government.

The separation of Church and State, although the mode involved injustice, has had the effect of stimulating both in behalf of popular education. There is no national university, but the people are learning to read. The few princely sees have disappeared, but the people sustain their clergy generously. A foreign political power no longer fills the bishoprics, but Rome has increased their number so as to bring religion more closely to the people. The first and most general result is, that the all but universal illiteracy of fifty years ago is rapidly diminishing. The schools are supported, partly by the national Government, partly by states and municipalities, partly by benevolent societies. Forty years ago the total sum expended on education by the Government could not have exceeded a hundred thousand dollars. Now it is more nearly five million dollars, if we include with the national appropriation the contributions from other sources, public and private. "With very few exceptions," says Janvier, "free schools, sustained by the state or municipal governments, the Church or benevolent societies, are found in all towns and villages; and in all the cities and larger towns, private schools are numerous. In the more important cities, colleges and professional schools are found. . . . Included in the general scheme are free night-schools for men and women, as well as schools in which trades are taught." It must be owned, however, that the history used in the schools gives a version of the American war with Mexico which would somewhat surprise Gen. Scott and the gallant lieutenants who fought with him.

A distinguished American economist,[1] who saw the country two years ago, says of the recent development of the educational spirit: —

"It is safe to say that more good, practical work has been done in this direction, within the last ten years, than in all of the preceding three hundred and fifty. At all of the important centres of population, free schools, under the auspices of the national Government, and free from all Church supervision, are reported as established; while the Catholic Church itself, stimulated, as it were, by its misfortunes, and apparently unwilling to longer rest under the imputation of having neglected education, is also giving much attention to the subject, and is said to be acting upon the principle of immediately establishing two schools wherever, in a given locality, the Government or any of the Protestant denominations establish one."

The Government also maintains national schools

[1] Mr. David A. Wells, like Mrs. Blake and the writer, was a member of the first Raymond excursion party which went from Boston over the Mexican Central. It would be imprudent, at least for the present, for women, or for men not fond of "roughing it," to make this delightful journey overland, except under experienced management such as we enjoyed, which charges itself with all responsibility for the traveller.

of agriculture, medicine, law, engineering, military science, music, and fine arts, as well as a national museum and a national library. The charitable and benevolent institutions, public and private, equal in number and scope, if they do not exceed, our own.

CHAPTER XII

REVENUE AND ITS APPLICATION

THERE is no danger that for many years to come, if ever, the prediction of Baron von Humboldt will be fulfilled, — that, with the advantage of good roads and free commerce, the Mexicans will one day undersell us in bread corn in the West Indies and other markets. Mexico has not yet good roads nor free commerce, nor, unless the tariff policy of the country shall be radically changed, can she have either. It is true that road-making in Switzerland is naturally no more difficult than in Mexico, if we omit the water-supply, — a very important factor in all industry. But the Romans and migratory Celts began making roads in Switzerland before, we may assume, Mexico had sent a sail out on the ocean; and the services which war rendered to peace in the Alps have been continually supplemented by the enlightened selfishness of a people who are animated in the cultivation of their soil by that highest incentive to industry, — ownership. No one who has travelled through Holland, over the bleak and all but sterile passes of the Juras, and across the Alps, can fail to realize that this incentive has made the agriculture of these countries what it is; while Ireland and Mexico, through millions of unused acres, and other millions under only slight cultivation, testify to the effect which landlordism, idle and oppressive, exercises over the most beneficent and indispensable among human industries.

Yet, without free commerce, and with roads, except the railroad lines, perhaps the worst in the world, and without machinery until within very recent times, the agriculture of Mexico under the republic has made extraordinary progress. In the portions of the valley which the Central Mexican traverses, there are regions with sufficient water. As a rule, irrigation is everywhere necessary. This fact should be remembered always in judging the Mexican people. The tenant who works land rents, not so many acres, but the right to so much water. In spite of this difficulty, the valley literally blossoms; and along the river-beds, few and not uniformly reliable, two, and sometimes three, crops a year are produced. The condition of the tenant, compared with what it was in the beginning of the century, has considerably improved. His lot then was like that of tenants elsewhere. The Mexican landlord got the tiller into debt, and then, giving him a little land for his own use, barely enough to raise the corn essential to life, made him and his family work out the debt in labor on the farm or hacienda.

It is a relief to find the Spaniards attempting to improve the status of these victims of imported feudalism. Las Casas and others drew the attention of the Spanish court to their sufferings: —

"The first attempt at amelioration was the *repartimientos de Indios*, by which they were divided among the Spaniards, who had the profits of their labor without a right to their persons; next the *encomiendas*, by which they were placed under the superintendence and protection of the Spaniards. The *encomendero* was bound to live in the district which contained the Indians of his *encomienda*, to watch over their conduct, instruct and civilize them, to protect them from all unjust persecutions, and to prevent their being imposed on in trafficking with the Spaniards. In return for these services, they received a tribute in labor or produce."[1]

These protectors, like the zemindars over the ryots in India, did precisely what might have been expected. No men can safely be intrusted with absolute power over the liberty or labor of other men. "The abuse of these protecting regulations followed closely their institution." The peonage, which existed legally in New Mexico until abolished by our Congress, was a relic of the "protecting" *encomiendas*. It actually exists in some parts of Mexico now; it must practically continue to exist, with varying degrees of enormity and oppression, until the idle-landlord system is abolished.

Over the greater part of the country under cultivation, the mode of farming is primitive. Near the larger cities, and especially on the lines of the railways, English and American machinery is coming into use, chiefly the reaper. But this can be true only of the rich haciendas. The tiller who has no capital, and receives for his share

[1] Notes on Mexico. 1824. London and Philadelphia.

NATIVE POPULATION

only a small fraction of the harvest, will neither buy machinery, nor, except along the railroads, can he rent it, since its transportation otherwise is next to impossible. Nor are the natives quick in using the railroads for local exchange of commodities. They continue to gaze upon the locomotive with awe, and they cling to old customs with a tenacity not free from disdain of the new ones. The men carry extraordinary burdens on their backs, and the small donkey is the favorite draught animal. The idea of raising foods for export has not yet crossed the brain of the vast bulk of the people. They undertake to raise enough for each year's local use; and so rigorous is the calculation, that, if a bad season come upon them, famine will be the consequence, unless the deficiency is supplied from the public granaries. It is to the credit of the Government that no appeals for aid are sent over the world. That distinction remains the undisputed dishonor of Great Britain. Poor as Mexico is, she has some sense of national decency.

If Nature has treated the country ill in failing to furnish roads, and in heaping up obstacles against their construction, thus impeding internal commerce, she has been no less parsimonious in indenting the coasts of Mexico with harbors for foreign trade. An official communication to our Government describes her coasts as broad belts of intolerable heat, disease, and aridity. On the whole coast-line there are but two natural harbors available for first-class modern merchant-vessels. But harbors can be made; whether natural or artificial, they do not create commerce. If the farmers of Mexico owned the tillable land; if the burden of taxation were shifted off industry upon land, proportionately to other property; if the tariff were so modified that commerce might freely seek Mexico, — harbors would not be wanting.

It is her mines that have kept up the foreign trade of Mexico in spite of her lack of harbors. The total value of her exports of precious metals annually from 1879 to 1884 averaged about twenty-five million dollars. But her total exports in 1885 have been estimated as high as forty-five million dollars, the increase being due in large measure to the closer relations brought about between our country and the sister republic by the new railroad lines. It is estimated that we received about fifty-five per cent of the total. The remainder was divided about as follows: England, 32.9; France, 4.8; Germany, 3; Spain, 2.6. The import trade of Mexico is the confession of her organic weakness. Its total value is about thirty-five million dollars, and consists of manufactured articles, which, for the most part, might be produced at home.

The Spaniards discouraged manufactures in Mexico for the benefit of their home industry; they did not prohibit them. But the want of steam or water power necessarily kept domestic manufacturing within small limits. Mayer records fifty-three cotton factories in 1844, running something more than one hundred and thirty thousand spindles. Mr. Wells found eighty-four factories returned by the tax-collectors in 1883, running something more than two hundred and forty thousand spindles. Mr. Titus Sheard, another of our pioneer party, himself a manufacturer, informed us, that, owing to the crude chemistry and rude methods, cotton costs nearly twice as much a yard in the Mexican mill as in the United States factories. The laborers employed are compelled to work from daylight to dark for little pay. Improved machinery and more modern processes would lower the cost of production materially. Meanwhile, a considerable quantity of manufactured cotton is imported, in spite of the excessive tariff. It was imported from Great Britain more largely in the past than from the United States. The railroads will probably alter that in time; but at present raw cotton may be carried by water from the Gulf to Liverpool, manufactured in Manchester, sent back to Vera Cruz, and thence by expensive rail to the capital, cheaper than from the United States to the same point. Another curious circumstance is, that although the cotton factories in Mexico have quadrupled in twenty years, and although the land around Querétaro and Orizaba, the chief cotton-making centres, is well suited to the growth of the plant, and it is actually grown there, New Orleans cotton is used exclusively at Orizaba, and one-half of that manufactured at Querétaro is also American. There is no reason why Mexico should not grow and manufacture all the cotton it requires.

The other manufactures of the country are trifling. The pottery, which has a reputation in excess of its merits, is at least adequate for the common uses of the people, whose culinary and other house habits are extremely primitive. Each family can be its own potter. The sewing-machine has given some impetus to the leather trade; but although the Mexican saddle is famous the world over, Mexico pays the United States nearly thirty thousand dollars a year for saddles, notwithstanding a duty of fifty-five per cent. This fact is accounted for in the superior mechanical appliances used by the American manufacturers.

It would appear at first sight that the devisors of the Mexican tariff had sought to rival Nature in producing artificial obstacles to match the physical ones. From the moment labor touches any article in Mexico, until it passes to the actual use of the consumer, it has hitherto been taxed. There was a time when it cost Spain forty-four per cent to collect the Crown revenues; her pernicious example has left this tradition of excessive taxation, and imposed the support of an army of tax-collectors upon the commerce of the country. Take a yard of calico. The land that produced the cotton pays nothing. The landlord has been the law-maker for Mexico, as he has been for Great Britain, Ireland, and India; as he was for Germany, until Stein and Hardenberg released the soil; as he was in France, until the Revolution. The land that produces the raw material pays nothing; but the instant labor touches it, cotton begins to pay taxes. Every thing used in transforming the boll into material is taxed: the dyes used in coloring it are taxed; the sale of each of them is individually taxed; the wagon that carts it from the field to the factory is taxed; the wheel that softens it is taxed; the animal that turns the wheel is taxed; the chemicals that enter into its composition are taxed; its transfer from the factor to the jobber is taxed; its transfer from the jobber to the retailer is taxed; its sale to the purchaser is taxed. Is it wonderful that cotton costs more at Orizaba and Querétaro than in Lowell or Manchester? It is not strange that more is not grown in Mexico. The merchant finds it more convenient to pay all his burdens at the custom-house, than each of the lot to the internal-revenue collectors.

This example may be slightly exaggerated, if taken literally. But the principle of Mexican taxation is fairly represented in it. The marvel is that so many blows in succession upon the arm of industry have not paralyzed it. A study of the Mexican tariff, with the phenomenon of trade increasing in spite of it, justifies the high expectations which sanguine Mexicans hold of the industrial future of their country. They say that this mode of raising national revenue must in time be remedied. They point out that remedial changes have already taken place. It was formerly the practice of the States to collect toll on every thing passing their borders, no matter what national taxes had already been paid. This interstate impost was prohibited a few years ago by Congress; but some of the States continued to enforce it, on the ground of necessity. It has been abolished by constitutional amendment.

The diminution of the national debt to a total of about one hundred and fifty million dollars, and the reduction of the number of civil servants, with a reduction also of the salaries of those retained, have put the national finances upon a safer and more hope-inspiring basis. The reduction of the tariff, both domestic and foreign, has followed quickly upon these happy achievements of the Diaz administration. The following articles are now on the free list at the custom-houses, where hitherto nearly every thing paid high duty : —

Barbed wire for fencing, hoes, bars for mines, fire-engines, hydraulic lime, printed books, all sorts of machinery, powder for mines, printing type, rags for paper, wire rope and cable, church clocks, and many useful chemicals.

Even the cockpit has paid a portion of the national revenue; and to the smiling cynic who may think too little of the politicians who condescend to this lowly and vicious source of money-making for national necessities, the reminder may be opportune, that to make the brutal who indulge in such sport pay for their pastime [1] is more tolerable to civilization than some methods of the governments of the Old World. Mexico raises revenue also by lotteries. The most pious of governments raised money in the same way

[1] I smile to recall that we were invited to occupy front seats, as a mark of honor, upon a certain Sunday evening, to witness this cruel and shocking spectacle. We were too timid or too super-refined to go. But when I read the other day the story of the evictions of Bodyke, Ire., where bedridden old women and half-naked children were thrown out into ditches; the roofs that sheltered them — in many cases built by their kindred — torn down, lest they should reclaim their own; and all this to extort by terror from others rents land and labor combined could not pay if the labor lived, the lottery, the bull-fight, and the cockpit, as means of making money, became civilized by comparison.

to help carry on the American war; it was only in 1823 that Great Britain went out of the gambling business. Every nation in Europe has indulged in it, with the exception (I think) of Russia. Paris resorts to a lottery to raise money for the illuminations on the national *fête*. States of the American Union derive revenue from gambling; and at least one American city swells its coffers from this source.

In the uses of the national revenue under the republic lies the clearest proof of the silent revolution. In 1808 Spain collected a total revenue of about twenty million dollars. Among the sources, by the way, were the monopoly of the sale of playing-cards, the tobacco monopoly, one-ninth of the tithes, the monopoly of gunpowder, sporting, gambling, the transfer of all kinds of commodities, a tax on the mines, a tax on papal dispensations, a tax on incomes of the inferior clergy, on stamps, and on ice. The portion nominally spent in Mexico, and not conveyed into the hands of the officials of the Crown, was probably one-fourth of the whole. It was expended chiefly on the army. Not a dollar appears to have been devoted to elementary education or useful public works. Marine docks were built one year, but they were reserved as arsenals. There were subsidies sent out to other Spanish colonies, and there were pensions for Crown favorites. This amount of revenue from a wretched population of about four millions and a half is amazing.

The revenue of the republic, with a population of at least ten millions, was in 1870, in round numbers, sixteen million dollars. In 1886-87 it reached thirty-two million dollars. The expenditures have kept pace with it, and in fact must have exceeded it, and must continue to exceed it for some years, until great public works are constructed, such as the drainage scheme already under contract, canals, bridges, roads, and harbors. The expenditure by departments presents a gratifying picture of national order and growth. The executive is the smallest item in the budget, only $49,252. Railway subventions have been liberally made; not as prodigally as in the case of our Pacific railways, but with a certainty of corresponding national benefit. Ten years ago Mexico had only four hundred miles of railway. There are now almost ten times as many. New York is distant from the ancient Aztec capital only six and a half days' journey. With the exception of the portion of the national debt which may have been unjustly assumed by the republic, every dollar of the revenue of Mexico is now applied to the development of the country. Progress is visible everywhere; and in every thing that enters into it, moral, political, and industrial, the influence of neighborhood is manifest.

It is true that the British bondholder is more successful in collecting interest on Mexican obligations than on Southern Confederacy paper, which he did so much to float for the sake of the interest; and it is true also that the capital invested in banking and in a considerable share of the mining enterprises of Mexico is English. But every day brings the sister republics closer. Every year effaces more of the old antagonism. English is supplanting French in the schools. In time it will make its way through the mountains with Spanish. It is certain that the war with Mexico was fought on a misunderstanding which the calmer sense of a later and more humane period would not repeat. The instincts of national self-interest prompt a policy of kindness and sincerity; a policy which shall respect the worthy traditions of an ancient and severely tried people, while it will promote a commercial communion certain to be mutually advantageous. Such a policy will hasten a commercial treaty just to both countries. The noble sentiment which should animate the nation of Washington, Lincoln, and Grant ought moreover to emphasize the approval of such a treaty by an act of grace, — the restoration of the flags and cannon captured by us in 1847. Nations not familiar with the precepts of Christianity were wont to make their war trophies, not of marble or metal, but of wood, that they might the more speedily perish. Why should we perpetuate the story of the defeat and humiliation of our sister republic?

IRENE E. JEROME'S • • • •
• • • • • • ART BOOKS

THE "PERPETUAL PLEASURE" SERIES

"The sketches are such as the most famous men of the country might be proud to own. They are original, strong, and impressive, even the lightest of them; and their variety, like a procession of Nature, is a perpetual pleasure."

A BUNCH OF VIOLETS. Original illustrations, engraved on wood and printed under the direction of GEORGE T. ANDREW. 4to, cloth, $3.75; Turkey morocco, $9.00; tree calf, $9.00; English seal style, $7.00.

The new volume is akin to the former triumphs of this favorite artist, whose "Sketch Books" have achieved a popularity unequalled in the history of fine art publications. In the profusion of designs, originality, and delicacy of treatment, the charming sketches of mountain, meadow, lake, and forest scenery of New England here reproduced are unexcelled. After the wealth of illustration which this student of nature has poured into the lap of art, to produce a volume in which there is no deterioration of power or beauty, but, if possible, increased strength and enlargement of ideas, gives assurance that the foremost female artist in America will hold the hearts of her legion of admirers.

NATURE'S HALLELUJAH. Presented in a series of nearly fifty full-page original illustrations (9½ x 14 inches), engraved on wood by GEORGE T. ANDREW. Elegantly bound in gold cloth, full gilt, gilt edges, $6.00; Turkey morocco, $12.00; tree calf, $12.00; English seal style, $10.00.

This volume has won the most cordial praise on both sides of the water. Mr. Francis H. Underwood, U. S. Consul at Glasgow, writes concerning it: "I have never seen anything superior, if equal, to the delicacy and finish of the engravings, and the perfection of the press-work. The copy you sent me has been looked over with evident and unfeigned delight by many people of artistic taste. Every one frankly says, 'It is impossible to produce such effects here,' and, whether it is possible or not, I am sure it is *not done;* no such effects are produced on this side of the Atlantic. In this combination of art and workmanship, the United States leads the world; and you have a right to be proud of the honor of presenting such a specimen to the public."

ONE YEAR'S SKETCH BOOK. Containing forty-six full-page original illustrations, engraved on wood by ANDREW; in same bindings and at same prices as "Nature's Hallelujah."

"Every thick, creamy page is embellished by some gems of art. Sometimes it is but a dash and a few trembling strokes; at others an impressive landscape, but in all and through all runs the master touch. Miss Jerome has the genius of an Angelo, and the execution of a Guido. The beauty of the sketches will be apparent to all, having been taken from our unrivalled New England scenery." — *Washington Chronicle.*

THE MESSAGE OF THE BLUEBIRD, Told to Me to Tell to Others. Original illustrations engraved on wood by ANDREW. Cloth and gold, $2.00; palatine boards, ribbon ornaments, $1.00.

"In its new bindings is one of the daintiest combinations of song and illustration ever published, exhibiting in a marked degree the fine poetic taste and wonderfully artistic touch which render this author's works so popular. The pictures are exquisite, and the verses exceedingly graceful, appealing to the highest sensibilities. The little volume ranks among the choicest of holiday souvenirs, and is beautiful and pleasing." — *Boston Transcript.*

Sold by all booksellers, and sent by mail, postpaid, on receipt of price

LEE AND SHEPARD Publishers Boston

NARRATIVES OF NOTED TRAVELLERS

GERMANY SEEN WITHOUT SPECTACLES; or, Random Sketches of Various Subjects, Penned from Different Standpoints in the Empire
By HENRY RUGGLES, late United States Consul at the Island of Malta, and at Barcelona, Spain. $1.50.
"Mr. Ruggles writes briskly: he chats and gossips, slashing right and left with stout American prejudices, and has made withal a most entertaining book." — *New-York Tribune.*

TRAVELS AND OBSERVATIONS IN THE ORIENT, with a Hasty Flight in the Countries of Europe
By WALTER HARRIMAN (ex-Governor of New Hampshire). $1.50.
"The author, in his graphic description of these sacred localities, refers with great aptness to scenes and personages which history has made famous. It is a chatty narrative of travel." — *Concord Monitor.*

FORE AND AFT
A Story of Actual Sea-Life. By ROBERT B. DIXON, M.D. $1.25.
Travels in Mexico, with vivid descriptions of manners and customs, form a large part of this striking narrative of a fourteen-months' voyage.

VOYAGE OF THE PAPER CANOE
A Geographical Journey of Twenty-five Hundred Miles from Quebec to the Gulf of Mexico. By NATHANIEL H. BISHOP. With numerous illustrations and maps specially prepared for this work. Crown 8vo. $1.50.
"Mr. Bishop did a very bold thing, and has described it with a happy mixture of spirit, keen observation, and *bonhomie.*" — *London Graphic.*

FOUR MONTHS IN A SNEAK-BOX
A Boat Voyage of Twenty-six Hundred Miles down the Ohio and Mississippi Rivers, and along the Gulf of Mexico. By NATHANIEL H. BISHOP. With numerous maps and illustrations. $1.50.
"His glowing pen-pictures of 'shanty-boat' life on the great rivers are true to life. His descriptions of persons and places are graphic." — *Zion's Herald.*

A THOUSAND MILES' WALK ACROSS SOUTH AMERICA, Over the Pampas and the Andes
By NATHANIEL H. BISHOP. Crown 8vo. New edition. Illustrated. $1.50.
"Mr. Bishop made this journey when a boy of sixteen, has never forgotten it, and tells it in such a way that the reader will always remember it, and wish there had been more."

CAMPS IN THE CARIBBEES
Being the Adventures of a Naturalist Bird-hunting in the West-India Islands. By FRED A. OBER. New edition. With maps and illustrations. $1.50.
"During two years he visited mountains, forests, and people, that few, if any, tourists had ever reached before. He carried his camera with him, and photographed from nature the scenes by which the book is illustrated." — *Louisville Courier-Journal.*

ENGLAND FROM A BACK WINDOW; With Views of Scotland and Ireland
By J. M. BAILEY, the "'Danbury News' Man." 12mo. $1.00.
"The peculiar humor of this writer is well known. The British Isles have never before been looked at in just the same way, — at least, not by any one who has notified us of the fact. Mr. Bailey's travels possess, accordingly, a value of their own for the reader, no matter how many previous records of journeys in the mother country he may have read." — *Rochester Express.*

Sold by all booksellers, and sent by mail, postpaid, on receipt of price

LEE AND SHEPARD Publishers Boston

YOUNG FOLKS' BOOKS OF TRAVEL

DRIFTING ROUND THE WORLD; A Boy's Adventures by Sea and Land

By CAPT. CHARLES W. HALL, author of "Adrift in the Ice-Fields," "The Great Bonanza," etc. With numerous full-page and letter-press illustrations. Royal 8vo. Handsome cover. $1.75. Cloth, gilt, $2.50.

"Out of the beaten track" in its course of travel, record of adventures, and descriptions of life in Greenland, Labrador, Ireland, Scotland, England, France, Holland, Russia, Asia, Siberia, and Alaska. Its hero is young, bold, and adventurous; and the book is in every way interesting and attractive.

EDWARD GREEY'S JAPANESE SERIES

YOUNG AMERICANS IN JAPAN; or, The Adventures of the Jewett Family and their Friend Oto Nambo

With 170 full-page and letter-press illustrations. Royal 8vo, 7 x 9½ inches. Handsomely illuminated cover. $1.75. Cloth, black and gold, $2.50.

This story, though essentially a work of fiction, is filled with interesting and truthful descriptions of the curious ways of living of the good people of the land of the rising sun.

THE WONDERFUL CITY OF TOKIO; or, The Further Adventures of the Jewett Family and their Friend Oto Nambo

With 169 illustrations. Royal 8vo, 7 x 9½ inches. With cover in gold and colors, designed by the author. $1.75. Cloth, black and gold, $2.50.

"A book full of delightful information. The author has the happy gift of permitting the reader to view things as he saw them. The illustrations are mostly drawn by a Japanese artist, and are very unique." —*Chicago Herald.*

THE BEAR WORSHIPPERS OF YEZO AND THE ISLAND OF KARAFUTO; being the further Adventures of the Jewett Family and their Friend Oto Nambo

180 illustrations. Boards, $1.75. Cloth, $2.50.

Graphic pen and pencil pictures of the remarkable bearded people who live in the north of Japan. The illustrations are by native Japanese artists, and give queer pictures of a queer people, who have been seldom visited.

HARRY W. FRENCH'S BOOKS

OUR BOYS IN INDIA

The wanderings of two young Americans in Hindustan, with their exciting adventures on the sacred rivers and wild mountains. With 145 illustrations. Royal 8vo, 7 x 9½ inches. Bound in emblematic covers of Oriental design, $1.75. Cloth, black and gold, $2.50.

While it has all the exciting interest of a romance, it is remarkably vivid in its pictures of manners and customs in the land of the Hindu. The illustrations are many and excellent.

OUR BOYS IN CHINA

The adventures of two young Americans, wrecked in the China Sea on their return from India, with their strange wanderings through the Chinese Empire. 188 illustrations. Boards, ornamental covers in colors and gold, $1.75. Cloth, $2.50.

This gives the further adventures of "Our Boys" of India fame in the land of Teas and Queues.

Sold by all booksellers, and sent by mail, postpaid, on receipt of price

LEE AND SHEPARD Publishers Boston

Bright and Breezy Books of Travel
— — — By Six Bright Women — — —

A WINTER IN CENTRAL AMERICA AND MEXICO
By HELEN J. SANBORN. Cloth, $1.50.
"A bright, attractive narrative by a wide-awake Boston girl."

A SUMMER IN THE AZORES, with a Glimpse of Madeira
By Miss C. ALICE BAKER. Little Classic style. Cloth, gilt edges, $1.25.
"Miss Baker gives us a breezy, entertaining description of these picturesque islands. She is an observing traveller, and makes a graphic picture of the quaint people and customs." — *Chicago Advance.*

LIFE AT PUGET SOUND
With sketches of travel in Washington Territory, British Columbia, Oregon, and California. By CAROLINE C. LEIGHTON. 16mo, cloth, $1.50.
"Your chapters on Puget Sound have charmed me. Full of life, deeply interesting, and with just that class of facts, and suggestions of truth, that cannot fail to help the Indian and the Chinese." — WENDELL PHILLIPS.

EUROPEAN BREEZES
By MARGERY DEANE. Cloth, gilt top, $1.50. Being chapters of travel through Germany, Austria, Hungary, and Switzerland, covering places not usually visited by Americans in making "the Grand Tour of the Continent," by the accomplished writer of "Newport Breezes."
"A very bright, fresh and amusing account, which tells us about a host of things we never heard of before, and is worth two ordinary books of European travel." — *Woman's Journal.*

BEATEN PATHS; or, A Woman's Vacation in Europe
By ELLA W. THOMPSON. 16mo, cloth. $1.50.
A lively and chatty book of travel, with pen-pictures humorous and graphic, that are decidedly out of the "beaten paths" of description.

AN AMERICAN GIRL ABROAD
By Miss ADELINE TRAFTON, author of "His Inheritance," "Katherine Earle," etc. 16mo. Illustrated. $1.50.
"A sparkling account of a European trip by a wide-awake, intelligent, and irrepressible American girl. Pictured with a freshness and vivacity that is delightful." — *Utica Observer.*

CURTIS GUILD'S TRAVELS

BRITONS AND MUSCOVITES; or, Traits of Two Empires
Cloth, $2.00.

OVER THE OCEAN; or, Sights and Scenes in Foreign Lands
By CURTIS GUILD, editor of "The Boston Commercial Bulletin." Crown 8vo. Cloth, $2.50.
"The utmost that any European tourist can hope to do is to tell the old story in a somewhat fresh way, and Mr. Guild has succeeded in every part of his book in doing this." — *Philadelphia Bulletin.*

ABROAD AGAIN; or, Fresh Forays in Foreign Fields
Uniform with "Over the Ocean." By the same author. Crown 8vo. Cloth, $2.50.
"He has given us a life-picture. Europe is done in a style that must serve as an invaluable guide to those who go 'over the ocean,' as well as an interesting companion." — *Halifax Citizen.*

Sold by all booksellers, and sent by mail, postpaid, on receipt of price

LEE AND SHEPARD Publishers Boston

A Library of Travel and Adventure in Foreign Lands

By Oliver Optic

Illustrated   Per Volume $1.50

YOUNG AMERICA ABROAD

First Series.

I. *OUTWARD BOUND;* OR, YOUNG AMERICA AFLOAT.

II. *SHAMROCK AND THISTLE;* OR, YOUNG AMERICA IN IRELAND AND SCOTLAND.

III. *RED CROSS;* OR, YOUNG AMERICA IN ENGLAND AND WALES.

IV. *DIKES AND DITCHES;* OR, YOUNG AMERICA IN HOLLAND AND BELGIUM.

V. *PALACE AND COTTAGE;* OR, YOUNG AMERICA IN FRANCE AND SWITZERLAND.

VI. *DOWN THE RHINE;* OR, YOUNG AMERICA IN GERMANY.

Second Series.

I. *UP THE BALTIC;* OR, YOUNG AMERICA IN NORWAY, SWEDEN, AND DENMARK.

II. *NORTHERN LANDS;* OR, YOUNG AMERICA IN RUSSIA AND PRUSSIA.

III. *CROSS AND CRESCENT;* OR, YOUNG AMERICA IN TURKEY AND GREECE.

IV. *SUNNY SHORES;* OR, YOUNG AMERICA IN ITALY AND AUSTRIA.

V. *VINE AND OLIVE;* OR, YOUNG AMERICA IN SPAIN AND PORTUGAL.

VI. *ISLES OF THE SEA;* OR, YOUNG AMERICA HOMEWARD BOUND.

Sold by all booksellers, and sent by mail, postpaid, on receipt of price.

LEE AND SHEPARD Publishers Boston

THE DOUGLAS NOVELS BY AMANDA M. DOUGLAS

A WOMAN'S INHERITANCE.
"Miss Douglas's Novels are all worth reading, and this is one full of suggestions, interesting situations, and bright dialogue."—*Cottage Hearth.*

OUT OF THE WRECK; or, Was it a Victory?
"Bright and entertaining as Miss Douglas's stories always are, this, her new one, leads them all."—*New Bedford Standard.*

FLOYD GRANDON'S HONOR.
"Fascinating throughout, and worthy of the reputation of the author."

WHOM KATHIE MARRIED.
Kathie was the heroine of the popular series of Kathie Stories for young people, the readers of which were very anxious to know with whom Kathie settled down in life. Hence this story, charmingly written.

LOST IN A GREAT CITY.
"There are the power of delineation and robustness of expression that would credit a masculine hand in the present volume."

THE OLD WOMAN WHO LIVED IN A SHOE.
"The romances of Miss Douglas's creation are all thrillingly interesting."—*Cambridge Tribune.*

HOPE MILLS; or, Between Friend and Sweetheart.
"Amanda Douglas is one of the favorite authors of American novel-readers."—*Manchester Mirror.*

FROM HAND TO MOUTH.
"There is real satisfaction in reading this book, from the fact that we can so readily 'take it home' to ourselves."—*Portland Argus.*

NELLY KINNARD'S KINGDOM.
"The Hartford Religious Herald" says, "This story is so fascinating, that one can hardly lay it down after taking it up."

IN TRUST; or, Dr. Bertrand's Household.
"She writes in a free, fresh and natural way, and her characters are never overdrawn."—*Manchester Mirror.*

CLAUDIA.
"The plot is very dramatic, and the *denouement* startling. Claudia, the heroine, is one of those self-sacrificing characters which it is the glory of the female sex to produce."—*Boston Journal.*

STEPHEN DANE.
"This is one of this author's happiest and most successful attempts at novel-writing, for which a grateful public will applaud her."—*Herald.*

HOME NOOK; or, The Crown of Duty.
"An interesting story of home-life, not wanting in incident, and written in forcible and attractive style."—*New York Graphic.*

SYDNIE ADRIANCE; or, Trying the World.
"The works of Miss Douglas have stood the test of popular judgment, and become the fashion."

SEVEN DAUGHTERS.
The charm of the story is the perfectly natural and home-like air which pervades it.

THE FORTUNES OF THE FARADAYS
"Of unexceptionable literary merit, deeply interesting in the development of the plot."—*Fall River News.*

FOES OF HER HOUSEHOLD.
"Full of interest from the first chapter to the end."

Sold by all booksellers, and sent by mail, post-paid, on receipt of price.

LEE AND SHEPARD, PUBLISHERS, BOSTON.

www.ingramcontent.com/pod-product-compliance
Lightning Source LLC
Chambersburg PA
CBHW021808230426
43669CB00008B/672